Krampusproofing Your Home

Krampusproofing Your Home

Matthew Petchinsky

Krampusproofing Your Home: Defensive Strategies for Yule
By: Matthew Petchinsky

Introduction: The Legend of Krampus and the Need for Defense
Overview of Krampus Folklore and Its Significance in Yule Traditions
In the shadowy tales of European winter folklore, few figures are as intriguing—or as terrifying—as Krampus. Known as the dark companion to St. Nicholas, Krampus is a horned, anthropomorphic figure whose name derives from the Old High German word *krampen*, meaning claw. This sinister creature roams the Alpine regions, striking fear into the hearts of children and adults alike during the Yule season.

While St. Nicholas rewards well-behaved children with gifts, Krampus serves as the enforcer of discipline. Often depicted with goat-like horns, cloven hooves, a long, serpentine tongue, and a bundle of birch branches in hand, Krampus punishes the naughty by whipping them, stuffing them into a sack, or, in the darkest tales, dragging them to his lair.

The origins of Krampus stretch back thousands of years to pre-Christian pagan traditions. He is believed to be a remnant of ancient winter solstice rituals, embodying the chaotic and wild forces of nature that demanded appeasement during the harshest time of year. As Christianity spread across Europe, Krampus became intertwined with St. Nicholas celebrations, particularly in Austria, Germany, and other parts of Central Europe. Today, Krampus remains a beloved (and feared) part of Yule festivities, with Krampusnacht (Krampus Night) observed on December 5th, the eve of St. Nicholas Day.

While the lore of Krampus can feel like an entertaining myth, for many it serves as a cautionary tale—a reminder of the need for balance between light and dark, kindness and mischief, discipline and indulgence. As modern Yule traditions evolve, Krampus persists as both a cultural symbol and a figure that inspires festive fear.

Why "Krampusproofing" Matters: Blending Myth, Tradition, and Practical Preparation

Though Krampus is steeped in myth, his enduring presence in Yule traditions reminds us that there's value in being prepared for the unexpected. Whether you view Krampus as a literal threat, a metaphor for winter's hardships, or a playful tradition, "Krampusproofing" your home serves multiple purposes.

- **Cultural Preservation:** Embracing the legend of Krampus allows us to connect with ancestral traditions and explore the rich tapestry of Yule customs. Preparing for Krampus becomes a way to honor these stories while adapting them for modern life.
- **Symbolic Balance:** The idea of warding off Krampus is more than just folklore; it symbolizes our efforts to protect our homes and families from the figurative "darkness" that winter can bring—whether that's illness, strife, or the challenges of the season.
- **Practical Benefits:** The strategies in this book not only "ward off Krampus" but also encourage mindfulness in creating a safe, welcoming, and harmonious home. From symbolic protections to physical security measures, "Krampusproofing" builds resilience against both mythical threats and real-world issues, like winter storms or unwelcome surprises during the holiday season.

This book bridges the gap between myth and practicality, providing readers with tools to both honor the legend of Krampus and create a safer, more festive Yule environment. By blending ancient wisdom with modern strategies, you'll gain insights into protecting your home in a way that's both meaningful and effective.

How to Use This Book: Understanding the Balance Between Folklore and Safety

"Krampusproofing Your Home" is more than just a guide to keeping the horned mischief-maker at bay—it's a manual for infusing your Yule celebrations with meaning, creativity, and a sense of security. This book is divided into six key sections, each designed to help you understand and prepare for Krampus in unique ways.

- **Understanding the Threat:** Begin with a thorough exploration of Krampus's lore, motives, and mythical behaviors to grasp the "why" behind the need for protection.
- **Defensive Preparations:** Learn how to fortify your home using a mix of folklore-inspired practices and practical security tips.
- **Active Defense Strategies:** Dive into hands-on methods for warding off Krampus, including rituals, charms, and tools that draw from ancient traditions.
- **Securing the Family:** Protecting your loved ones is a central theme, with chapters dedicated to educating children, fortifying family spaces, and involving pets in your defensive plans.
- **Fortifying the Spirit:** Discover spiritual and ritualistic practices that help strengthen the intangible defenses of your home, creating a space of peace and positivity.

- Aftermath and Reassurance: Should Krampus "visit," you'll find tips for cleansing, healing, and preparing for the next Yule season.

The book is written with a balance of lightheartedness and seriousness. While it's fun to embrace the playful fear of Krampus, the preparations detailed here also provide valuable lessons for cultivating a safe and joyful Yule. You'll find practical guides, cultural insights, and creative rituals to make your holidays memorable and protected.

Throughout the chapters, keep in mind the spirit of Yule—a celebration of light in the darkest time of year. By blending tradition with modern strategies, you'll ensure your home remains a sanctuary, keeping Krampus (and other unwelcome forces) at bay. Let's begin the journey to Krampusproofing your home and making this Yule season both safe and magical.

Part I: Understanding the Threat

Chapter 1: Who is Krampus?

The Origins of Krampus

Krampus, the dark counterpart to the benevolent St. Nicholas, has roots that extend deep into European folklore, with origins believed to predate Christianity. The name "Krampus" derives from the Old High German word *krampen*, meaning "claw," a fitting descriptor for this fearsome figure. Often associated with the Alpine regions of Europe, Krampus embodies the chaotic and untamed forces of nature, acting as a harbinger of discipline during the Yule season.

Scholars trace Krampus's lineage to ancient pagan traditions, particularly those of the pre-Christian winter solstice festivals. These celebrations often involved figures that represented the duality of the season: the abundance and joy of harvests contrasted with the looming hardships of winter. Krampus is thought to be a remnant of these rituals, embodying the darker, wilder forces that demanded recognition and appeasement during this time of year.

One theory links Krampus to the Norse god Hel, ruler of the underworld, whose domain encompassed death and chaos. Another posits connections to the horned fertility deities of ancient pagan practices, such as the Greek god Pan or the Celtic Cernunnos. These deities were often depicted as part-human, part-animal beings, symbolizing the primal and untamed aspects of life.

As Christianity spread through Europe, pagan figures like Krampus were not eradicated but rather assimilated into the new religious framework. Krampus, once a symbol of untamed chaos, became a companion to St. Nicholas, representing the darker aspects of morality and discipline in contrast to the saint's generosity and kindness.

The Myths of Krampus

The mythology of Krampus is as varied as the regions in which his legend is told. Central to his story is his role as an enforcer of discipline, punishing those who fail to meet the moral standards of the season. Traditionally, Krampus is said to roam the streets on the night of December 5th—known as *Krampusnacht* (Krampus Night)—to seek out naughty children.

Krampus is typically described as a horned, goat-like creature with sharp claws, glowing red eyes, and a long, pointed tongue. His body is covered in coarse black or brown fur, and he often carries a bundle of birch branches, called *ruten*, used to swat misbehaving children. In some tales, he also carries a sack or a large basket on his back to abduct particularly unruly children, taking them to his lair—or, in more gruesome versions, to the underworld.

The juxtaposition of Krampus and St. Nicholas creates a moral dichotomy: while St. Nicholas rewards good behavior with gifts and treats, Krampus delivers swift and terrifying justice to those who fail to meet the season's expectations. This dynamic reflects a deep cultural tradition of teaching morality through the interplay of reward and punishment.

Cultural Variations of Krampus Across Europe
While the figure of Krampus is most closely associated with Austria and Germany, variations of his legend appear across Europe, each region adding its own unique flair to the myth.

- **Austria and Germany**
  In Austria and Germany, Krampus is a central figure in Christmas celebrations. The traditional *Krampuslauf* (Krampus Run) is a public parade where participants dress as Krampus and roam the streets, playfully scaring onlookers. These events blend festive cheer with an air of fear, embodying the spirit of Krampusnacht.
- **Slovenia**
  In Slovenia, Krampus is known as *Parkelj* and shares many similarities with his Austrian counterpart. However, the focus is often placed on his role as a helper to St. Nicholas, emphasizing the balance between good and evil in holiday traditions.
- **Hungary**
  In Hungary, a similar figure called *Krampusz* is part of St. Nicholas Day celebrations. The Hungarian version is often depicted as more mischievous than malevolent, focusing on scaring children rather than physically punishing them.
- **Czech Republic and Slovakia**
  In these regions, Krampus is part of the broader folklore of *Mikuláš* (St. Nicholas), accompanied by other figures like angels and devils. The devil-like aspect of Krampus is emphasized here, aligning him with broader Christian concepts of sin and punishment.
- **Italy**
  In Italy, particularly in the Tyrol region, Krampus is known as *Krampuš*. He appears during local St. Nicholas processions, maintaining his role as a punisher of the naughty. Italian Krampus often has more ornate costumes, reflecting the region's artistic traditions.
- **France**
  In Alsace and Lorraine, Krampus takes on the guise of *Père Fouettard* (Father Whipper). This figure, while less demonic in appearance, serves a similar purpose, punishing misbehavior with a switch or whip.
- **Scandinavia**
  In Scandinavian countries, while Krampus as a named figure is less prevalent, there are similar traditions involving Yule spirits or trolls who punish the naughty and reward the good.

The Evolution of Krampus in Modern Times

In recent years, Krampus has experienced a revival beyond his traditional Alpine roots. The creature has become a global symbol of the darker side of Christmas, celebrated in art, literature, films, and even merchandise. Krampuslauf events have spread to cities across the world, bringing the eerie yet festive tradition to new audiences.

This resurgence has sparked a renewed interest in understanding Krampus's cultural significance. For some, he is a figure of fear and discipline; for others, he represents a playful rebellion against the commercialization of Christmas. His presence serves as a reminder of the moral lessons embedded in holiday traditions, as well as the balance of light and dark that defines the Yule season.

Conclusion

Krampus is far more than just a Christmas villain; he is a rich and complex figure deeply embedded in the cultural fabric of Europe. His story has evolved over centuries, blending pagan and Christian elements into a myth that continues to captivate and terrify. By understanding the origins, myths, and variations of Krampus, we gain insight into the ways cultures use storytelling to navigate the dualities of life—good and evil, joy and fear, reward and punishment. As you embark on this journey to Krampusproof your home, remember that the legend of Krampus is as much about balance as it is about protection.

Chapter 2: Signs of a Krampus Visit
Common Folklore Indicators and Symbolic Warnings
The Mysterious Presence of Krampus: Recognizing the Signs

In folklore, Krampus is not just a physical presence but also a symbolic force that manifests through eerie signs and omens. Recognizing the indicators of a Krampus visit requires a keen eye for subtle details and an understanding of the myth's deeper meanings. This chapter will guide you through the common folklore warnings that signal Krampus may be near.

1. Physical Signs in the Environment

Krampus is said to leave behind distinct physical markers, many of which are rooted in the myths and traditions of Alpine folklore. These signs often serve as a warning to prepare for his arrival or as evidence that he has already visited.

- **Cloven Hoofprints in the Snow**
  One of the most common signs of Krampus's presence is cloven hoofprints, often appearing mysteriously in freshly fallen snow or muddy ground near a home. These tracks may lead to the door of a household or circle the property, symbolizing that Krampus is assessing his potential "targets."
- **Discarded Birch Branches**
  Birch branches, known as *ruten*, are a signature tool of Krampus, used to swat naughty children. Finding these branches near your home, especially freshly broken or scorched at the tips, is considered a sure sign that Krampus has been nearby.
- **Scorched or Burned Marks**
  Krampus is often associated with fire and brimstone, a nod to his underworld origins. His visits are sometimes marked by faint scorch marks on doorways, windowsills, or even floors, as if he has passed through with a fiery touch.

2. Unusual Noises and Auditory Warnings

Krampus is not a quiet visitor. Folklore describes his approach as accompanied by a cacophony of sounds that instill fear in those who hear them.

- **Clanking Chains**
  Krampus is often depicted carrying heavy chains, which he drags behind him as he roams. The sound of chains scraping against the ground or rattling in the distance is a classic warning of his approach.
- **Bell Chimes**
  In some traditions, Krampus carries bells to announce his presence. These bells have a distinctive tone, described as deeper and more foreboding than ordinary sleigh bells. Hearing these chimes, particularly at odd hours, is a chilling sign.

- **Low Growls or Grunts**

  Folklore often describes Krampus as emitting guttural growls, grunts, or even snorts reminiscent of a wild beast. These noises are said to come from just beyond the edge of human visibility, adding to the fear of his unseen presence.

3. Strange Weather Patterns

Krampus is sometimes associated with sudden and unexplainable changes in the weather. These shifts are often seen as nature responding to his malevolent energy.

- **Sudden, Bitter Cold**

  While winter is naturally cold, folklore describes an unnatural chill that accompanies Krampus. This icy blast is often described as penetrating, even when one is indoors.

- **Thick Fog or Mist**

  Krampus is believed to shroud himself in dense fog or mist, obscuring his movements and creating an eerie atmosphere. This weather phenomenon is often reported during *Krampusnacht* or near homes he has visited.

4. Behavioral Changes in Animals

Animals are said to be particularly sensitive to Krampus's presence, reacting in ways that serve as a warning to their human companions.

- **Restless Pets**

  Dogs may bark incessantly at unseen entities, cats may hiss or hide, and livestock may become agitated for no apparent reason. These behaviors often escalate as Krampus draws nearer.

- **Missing Livestock**

  In some tales, Krampus is said to target not just naughty children but also livestock as a form of punishment for families. Missing or mysteriously harmed animals can be a sign of his wrath.

5. Supernatural Occurrences and Symbolic Warnings

Beyond the physical and auditory signs, Krampus's visits are often marked by supernatural phenomena and symbolic warnings that defy rational explanation.

- **Shadowy Figures**

  Krampus is said to linger on the edges of visibility, appearing as a dark, hulking figure in the shadows. Sightings of such figures near windows, doorways, or in the woods are considered ominous.

- **Flickering Lights**

  Lights that flicker or extinguish without cause are another sign of Krampus's presence. This is often interpreted as a disruption of the protective energies in a home.

- **Unexplained Smells**
  The scent of sulfur or burning wood, especially when no fire is present, is said to herald Krampus's approach, linking him to his infernal origins.

6. The Emotional Atmosphere of the Home

Krampus's presence is not only felt in the physical world but also in the emotional and spiritual atmosphere of a household.

- **Heightened Tensions**
  Families often report an increase in arguments, misbehavior, or general unease before a suspected Krampus visit. This aligns with the legend that Krampus is drawn to disorder and negativity.
- **A Sense of Being Watched**
  Many tales describe an overwhelming feeling of being observed, as if unseen eyes are scrutinizing every action. This sensation is often accompanied by chills or an unshakable sense of dread.

7. Dreams and Nightmares

In some traditions, Krampus is said to invade the dreams of those he targets, particularly children.

- **Recurring Nightmares**
  Children may report vivid dreams of being chased, captured, or punished by a horned figure. These nightmares often leave them waking in fear, unable to return to sleep.
- **Visions of Birch Branches or Chains**
  Adults, too, may experience unsettling dreams involving Krampus's signature tools, interpreting them as warnings to mend their ways.

Responding to the Signs

If you notice any of these signs, folklore suggests immediate action to protect your home and loved ones. This may include lighting protective candles, placing wards or charms at entry points, or performing rituals to banish negative energies. These strategies, explored in later chapters, are designed to create a barrier between Krampus and your household.

While these signs may sound fantastical, they serve an important symbolic purpose. They remind us to reflect on our actions, repair relationships, and create harmony within our homes during the Yule season. Whether you see Krampus as a literal threat or a metaphorical one, recognizing and addressing these warnings ensures that your Yule celebrations remain safe and joyous.

By understanding the signs of a Krampus visit, you are better prepared to take the next steps in Krampusproofing your home. Let us now delve into the preparations necessary to keep this shadowy figure at bay.

Chapter 3: The Psychology of Krampus
Exploring the Mythological Motives Behind His Actions
Introduction: The Complexity of Krampus's Role

Krampus is more than a frightening figure meant to scare children into good behavior; he embodies a profound duality and serves as a symbolic mirror for human behavior, morality, and the interplay between order and chaos. Understanding the psychology of Krampus requires delving into the mythological underpinnings that shape his actions. Why does Krampus punish? What drives his terrifying pursuits? This chapter explores the motivations behind Krampus's behavior, revealing a character that is as complex as the traditions surrounding him.

1. Krampus as the Enforcer of Discipline

One of the most consistent themes in Krampus lore is his role as a disciplinarian. While St. Nicholas rewards virtue, Krampus enforces morality by punishing misbehavior. This dynamic reflects an age-old human need to balance reward and consequence.

- **A Symbol of Consequences**

  Krampus serves as a cautionary figure, reminding children and adults alike that actions have repercussions. His punishments, from symbolic swats with birch branches to the more sinister abductions in folklore, are designed to instill a sense of accountability.

- **The Duality of Reward and Punishment**

  By juxtaposing Krampus with St. Nicholas, the myth reinforces the dual forces of life: kindness and discipline, light and dark, reward and retribution. This duality is central to the human experience and has been used in countless cultures to teach morality.

- **A Catalyst for Reflection**

  In punishing the naughty, Krampus pushes individuals to reflect on their behavior. His terrifying presence forces people to confront their own actions and make amends, reinforcing the importance of self-awareness and growth.

2. The Archetype of Chaos and Fear

Krampus's monstrous appearance and fearsome actions place him firmly within the archetype of chaos—a necessary counterbalance to the order represented by St. Nicholas. This archetypal role sheds light on the psychological and cultural need for figures like Krampus.

- **Channeling Collective Fears**

  Krampus acts as a vessel for the collective fears of society, particularly those associated with the uncertainties of winter. The harsh realities of the season—scarcity, cold, and darkness—are embodied in his wild, untamed persona.

- **The Role of Fear in Moral Education**

  Fear, while uncomfortable, is a powerful motivator. Krampus's frightening presence is not meant to traumatize but to serve as a stark reminder of the consequences of straying from moral paths. This aligns with the broader human use of fear as a tool for teaching and enforcing cultural norms.

- **The Need for Chaos in Order**
  Psychologically, Krampus represents the chaotic forces that exist alongside order. His presence acknowledges that darkness and mischief are inevitable parts of the human experience and must be faced rather than ignored.

3. Krampus and the Shadow Self

Krampus can be seen as a manifestation of the human shadow, a concept introduced by psychologist Carl Jung. The shadow represents the darker, repressed aspects of the psyche that society often deems unacceptable.

- **A Mirror to Our Darkest Impulses**
  Krampus embodies the anger, mischief, and unrestrained desires that exist within every individual. By externalizing these traits, the myth allows people to confront and address them in a safe, symbolic way.
- **Confronting the Shadow Through Myth**
  The legend of Krampus provides a framework for integrating the shadow self. By acknowledging Krampus's role in punishing misdeeds, individuals are encouraged to take responsibility for their own darker tendencies and work toward self-improvement.
- **The Catharsis of Fear**
  The fear Krampus invokes can be cathartic, allowing individuals to experience and release pent-up anxieties. This emotional purge reinforces psychological balance and helps individuals emerge stronger.

4. The Cultural Context of Punishment

The psychological motives behind Krampus's actions are deeply tied to the cultural context in which his legend developed. Understanding these cultural influences provides insight into why Krampus punishes and what his punishments signify.

- **Winter as a Time of Reflection**
  In the harsh winters of Alpine Europe, survival depended on cooperation, discipline, and foresight. Krampus's punishments reflect the cultural need to enforce these values during the Yule season, ensuring that communities remained united and prepared for the challenges ahead.
- **The Importance of Social Order**
  Krampus reinforces societal norms by targeting those who deviate from them. His actions serve as a warning against selfishness, greed, and disobedience, qualities that could jeopardize the cohesion of a small, tight-knit community.
- **The Ritualized Nature of Punishment**
  Krampus's actions are not random but ritualized, following a predictable pattern that aligns

with the seasonal cycle. This ritualization makes his punishments less about individual malice and more about upholding communal values.

5. Krampus and the Innocent

While Krampus's primary focus is on punishing the naughty, his relationship with innocence is complex. Folklore suggests that Krampus has a grudging respect for purity and virtue, even as he terrorizes those who fall short.

- **A Protector of Virtue**
  By punishing wrongdoers, Krampus indirectly protects those who are virtuous. His actions ensure that the values of honesty, kindness, and discipline are upheld, creating a safer environment for the innocent.
- **The Line Between Fear and Play**
  In modern celebrations like *Krampuslauf* (Krampus Run), Krampus interacts with children and adults in ways that are both frightening and playful. This duality underscores his role as a figure who disciplines without malice, emphasizing the importance of balance.

6. The Mythological Need for Balance

Krampus's existence highlights a fundamental psychological and mythological truth: the need for balance between opposing forces.

- **Light Cannot Exist Without Darkness**
  The legend of Krampus reminds us that goodness (St. Nicholas) cannot truly be appreciated without its counterpart, darkness (Krampus). This balance reflects the cyclical nature of life, where joy and hardship coexist.
- **A Reflection of Inner Balance**
  On a personal level, Krampus challenges individuals to achieve their own balance between virtue and vice. His presence pushes people to reflect on their actions and strive for self-improvement, fostering personal growth.

Conclusion: The Purpose of Krampus's Punishments

Krampus is not simply a villain or an agent of chaos—he is a necessary force within the mythological framework of Yule. His punishments are not acts of cruelty but tools for teaching, reflection, and balance. By exploring the psychology of Krampus, we uncover a deeper understanding of his role in shaping human behavior, morality, and cultural traditions. As we move forward in this book, keep in mind that Krampus's actions, though fearsome, are rooted in a desire to uphold balance and harmony in the world. This understanding will guide your efforts to protect your home while honoring the lessons Krampus has to teach.

Part II: Defensive Preparations

Chapter 4: Krampus vs. Santa: A Tale of Duality
Understanding Their Relationship in Folklore and What It Means for Modern Yule
Introduction: The Duality of Krampus and Santa

The pairing of Krampus and Santa Claus (or St. Nicholas) represents one of the most iconic and fascinating dualities in folklore. While Santa embodies generosity, kindness, and the reward for virtuous behavior, Krampus is his dark counterpart, meting out punishment to those who fall short of societal expectations. Together, they create a symbolic balance, highlighting the coexistence of light and dark, reward and punishment, and order and chaos.

This duality is not just a relic of folklore but a framework that continues to shape modern Yule traditions. Understanding their relationship offers insight into the values these myths aim to convey and the enduring relevance of their symbolic partnership.

1. The Origins of Santa and Krampus as Complementary Figures

- **St. Nicholas: The Archetype of Generosity**
  The figure of Santa Claus originates from St. Nicholas, a 4th-century Christian bishop known for his acts of charity and kindness. St. Nicholas became the patron saint of children and sailors, celebrated for his miraculous deeds and his willingness to help the needy. His feast day, December 6th, became a time for giving and joy.
- **Krampus: The Pagan Enforcer of Discipline**
  Krampus, by contrast, has roots in pre-Christian pagan traditions, where he served as a symbol of nature's wild and chaotic forces. As Christianity spread, Krampus was integrated into St. Nicholas celebrations, transforming from a pagan entity to a moral enforcer in Christian folklore. His role became that of punishing those who failed to embody the virtues St. Nicholas rewarded.
- **A Symbolic Partnership**
  The partnership of Krampus and St. Nicholas reflects a broader cultural need for balance. Together, they embody the dual forces of kindness and discipline, reinforcing the moral structure of society. This pairing ensured that both positive and negative behaviors were acknowledged during the Yule season.

2. The Mythological Significance of Duality

The relationship between Krampus and Santa reflects a universal mythological theme: the duality of light and dark. This concept appears in numerous cultural traditions and serves as a way to understand and navigate the complexities of life.

- **Light vs. Dark**
  Santa and Krampus represent the eternal struggle between light and dark. Santa's light brings joy, warmth, and generosity, while Krampus's darkness invokes fear, discipline, and introspection. Their coexistence reminds us that one cannot exist without the other.

- Order vs. Chaos
  Santa is a figure of order, spreading joy and maintaining harmony. Krampus, on the other hand, embodies chaos, disrupting complacency and forcing individuals to confront their shortcomings. This dynamic mirrors the natural balance between stability and change.
- Reward vs. Punishment
  By rewarding the good and punishing the bad, Santa and Krampus reinforce the moral duality inherent in human society. This pairing serves as a tool for teaching accountability, ensuring that both virtue and vice are addressed during the Yule season.

3. How Krampus and Santa Work Together in Folklore

Despite their stark differences, Krampus and Santa share a symbiotic relationship that enhances the effectiveness of their roles in folklore.

- The Division of Labor
  In many traditions, Krampus acts as the "bad cop" to Santa's "good cop." While Santa rewards good children with gifts and treats, Krampus ensures that those who misbehave face consequences. This division of labor allows them to address the full spectrum of human behavior.
- Balancing Fear and Joy
  The pairing of Krampus and Santa creates an emotional balance. While Santa's presence inspires joy and excitement, Krampus invokes fear and caution. Together, they ensure that the Yule season is both festive and reflective.
- A Unified Moral Message
  By working together, Krampus and Santa deliver a cohesive moral message: good behavior is rewarded, but bad behavior has consequences. This dual approach makes the lessons of Yule more impactful and memorable.

4. The Evolution of Krampus and Santa in Modern Times

As cultural attitudes have shifted, so too have the roles of Krampus and Santa. Their relationship continues to evolve, reflecting changing values and traditions.

- Santa's Commercialization
  In modern times, Santa Claus has become a symbol of commercialized Christmas, focusing on gift-giving, consumerism, and festive cheer. This shift has somewhat diluted his original role as a moral arbiter, leaving Krampus's role as the punisher more pronounced in certain traditions.
- The Revival of Krampus
  In contrast to Santa's commercialization, Krampus has seen a resurgence in popularity as a symbol of rebellion against overly sanitized holiday traditions. Events like

Krampuslauf (Krampus Runs) celebrate his mischievous and chaotic nature, reminding people of the darker, wilder aspects of Yule.

- Pop Culture Representations
  Both Krampus and Santa have become fixtures in pop culture, appearing in movies, books, and art. These representations often highlight their duality, with Santa as the benevolent giver and Krampus as the fearsome enforcer.

5. What the Duality of Krampus and Santa Teaches Us

The enduring appeal of Krampus and Santa lies in the lessons their duality imparts. These figures serve as mirrors for our own experiences and values, offering timeless wisdom for navigating life.

- The Importance of Accountability
  Santa and Krampus remind us that our actions have consequences. By rewarding good behavior and punishing bad, they encourage personal accountability and self-reflection.
- The Necessity of Balance
  The pairing of light and dark, reward and punishment, emphasizes the need for balance in life. Both joy and fear play essential roles in shaping our experiences and guiding our actions.
- Embracing Complexity
  The coexistence of Santa and Krampus teaches us to embrace the complexity of human nature. We are capable of both kindness and mischief, and acknowledging both aspects of ourselves is key to personal growth.

Conclusion: The Modern Meaning of Krampus and Santa

The tale of Krampus and Santa is more than just a story for the Yule season; it is a profound reflection of human nature and societal values. Their duality serves as a reminder that life is a balance of opposites, where light and dark, joy and fear, must coexist.

In modern celebrations, this duality can inspire us to reflect on our own behaviors and strive for a harmonious balance. As you continue your journey through this book, remember that both Santa's generosity and Krampus's discipline have a role to play in creating a meaningful and protected Yule season. By understanding their relationship, you are better equipped to embrace the full spectrum of Yule traditions, ensuring a holiday that is both joyful and reflective.

Chapter 5: Assessing Your Home's Vulnerabilities
Identifying Entry Points and Weaknesses Krampus Might Exploit
Introduction: The Importance of Fortifying Your Home

In folklore, Krampus is a cunning figure capable of finding his way into even the most secure homes. Though his mythical nature might seem intangible, the symbolic act of "Krampusproofing" your home provides practical and psychological benefits. By addressing vulnerabilities, you not only protect against his folkloric presence but also create a safer, more secure environment for your family during the Yule season. This chapter will guide you through identifying potential weaknesses in your home and fortifying them to ensure your holiday celebrations remain safe and harmonious.

1. Understanding Krampus's Methods

To effectively protect your home, it's important to understand how Krampus operates according to folklore. Stories often describe him as being both physically imposing and supernaturally cunning, capable of exploiting physical, emotional, and spiritual weaknesses.

- **Physical Entry Points: Krampus is said to gain access through chimneys, doors, windows, and other common openings, much like Santa Claus but with far more sinister intentions.**
- **Supernatural Abilities: Some myths attribute Krampus with the power to bypass physical barriers, appearing suddenly in the shadows or manifesting wherever there is mischief or negativity.**
- **Emotional Exploitation: Krampus is drawn to households rife with discord, misbehavior, or a lack of holiday spirit. Identifying and addressing these vulnerabilities is as important as securing physical entry points.**

2. Assessing Physical Entry Points

Start by inspecting your home for physical vulnerabilities that Krampus—or, in a practical sense, any unwanted visitor—might exploit.

Chimneys

- **Traditional Symbolism: In many Krampus legends, he uses chimneys as his primary entry point, mirroring Santa's mode of arrival.**
- **Practical Vulnerabilities:**
    - **Open or uncapped chimneys allow not only Krampus but also cold drafts, pests, and debris to enter.**
    - **Creosote buildup or structural damage makes chimneys a fire hazard.**
- **Solutions:**
    - **Install a chimney cap to block unwanted entry.**
    - **Schedule a professional chimney cleaning and inspection before the Yule season.**

Doors

- **Traditional Symbolism:** Doors represent the threshold between safety and external chaos, making them key targets for Krampus.
- **Practical Vulnerabilities:**
  - Weak locks, broken frames, or poorly sealed doors can be easily breached.
  - Sliding glass doors and back doors are often overlooked and less secure.
- **Solutions:**
  - Upgrade locks to deadbolts or smart locks for added security.
  - Reinforce door frames and install weather stripping to eliminate drafts and gaps.
  - Use door jammers or security bars for sliding doors.

Windows

- **Traditional Symbolism:** Windows are often described in folklore as the eyes of the home, making them a target for Krampus's watchful gaze.
- **Practical Vulnerabilities:**
  - Cracked glass, poorly latching locks, or missing screens invite intruders.
  - Windows left open or unlocked are an easy access point.
- **Solutions:**
  - Install sturdy locks or security latches on all windows.
  - Consider window security film or shatter-resistant glass for added protection.
  - Keep curtains or blinds closed during nighttime to block prying eyes.

Attics and Basements

- **Traditional Symbolism:** These spaces are often associated with hiding secrets or neglect, making them symbolic weak spots for Krampus.
- **Practical Vulnerabilities:**
  - Attic vents or basement windows are frequently unsecured and forgotten.
  - Neglected areas attract pests and reduce overall home security.
- **Solutions:**
  - Inspect vents and basement windows, sealing any gaps or installing mesh barriers.
  - Keep these spaces clean and well-lit to deter unwanted attention.

Garages

- **Traditional Symbolism:** The garage, as an extension of the home, represents a transitional space that is often less protected.

- Practical Vulnerabilities:
    ◦ Weak or outdated garage doors can be easily forced open.
    ◦ Internal doors connecting the garage to the main house are often not reinforced.
- Solutions:
    ◦ Install a modern, reinforced garage door with automatic locks.
    ◦ Upgrade the door between the garage and the house to one with a deadbolt.

3. Addressing Emotional and Energetic Vulnerabilities

In folklore, Krampus is drawn to emotional discord and negative energy. Addressing these vulnerabilities is as important as securing physical entry points.

Family Tensions

- Mythical Perspective: Krampus is said to target households rife with misbehavior or a lack of holiday spirit.
- Practical Implications:
    ◦ Arguments and unresolved conflicts create an atmosphere of negativity.
    ◦ Disengagement from Yule traditions weakens the household's symbolic protections.
- Solutions:
    ◦ Foster open communication and resolve conflicts before the holidays.
    ◦ Engage in shared holiday activities like decorating, baking, or storytelling to strengthen familial bonds.

Neglected Traditions

- Mythical Perspective: Houses that fail to honor the Yule season's customs are more vulnerable to Krampus.
- Practical Implications:
    ◦ Skipping rituals or celebrations can lead to a sense of disconnection and vulnerability.
- Solutions:
    ◦ Incorporate meaningful traditions, such as lighting Yule candles or hanging protective symbols like wreaths and bells.

Negative Energy in the Home

- Mythical Perspective: Krampus is often drawn to spaces filled with unresolved negativity.
- Practical Implications:
    ◦ Clutter, poor lighting, and stagnant air can create an oppressive atmosphere.

- Solutions:
  - Clean and declutter the home, focusing on corners and forgotten spaces.
  - Use aromatherapy or incense with protective scents like frankincense, cedar, or pine.

4. Strengthening the Boundaries of Your Home

Once vulnerabilities have been identified, take steps to reinforce your home's physical and symbolic boundaries.

- **Protective Wards and Charms**
  Place protective symbols, such as pentagrams, runes, or sigils, at entry points to ward off negative energies. In folklore, bells, wreaths, and holly are also considered powerful deterrents against Krampus.
- **Lighting the Perimeter**
  Use outdoor lights to illuminate dark areas around your home. Motion-activated lights are particularly effective in deterring both mythical and real intruders.
- **Creating a Protective Atmosphere**
  Decorate with symbols of joy and protection, such as candles, evergreen garlands, and Yule ornaments. These elements not only enhance the holiday spirit but also create an environment that is uninviting to malevolent forces.

5. Preparing for the Unexpected

Despite your best efforts, no home is completely impervious to threats. Preparing for the unexpected ensures that you can respond effectively to any situation.

- **Emergency Supplies**
  Keep flashlights, batteries, and a first-aid kit readily accessible in case of power outages or other emergencies.
- **Safety Drills**
  Practice evacuation or lockdown procedures with your family to ensure everyone knows what to do in case of an emergency.
- **Spiritual Safeguards**
  Have protective rituals or prayers prepared for use in moments of heightened tension or fear.

Conclusion: Securing Your Home, Strengthening Your Spirit

Assessing your home's vulnerabilities is the first step in Krampusproofing your space. By addressing physical entry points, emotional tensions, and energetic imbalances, you create a sanctuary that is safe not only from mythical threats but also from real-world challenges. As you move forward in this guide, remember that the act of fortifying your home is as much about fostering a sense of security and harmony as it is about physical protection. With these measures in place, you'll be ready to face whatever the Yule season brings—Krampus included.

Chapter 6: Yule Wards and Charms
Creating Effective Magical and Symbolic Deterrents
Introduction: The Protective Power of Yule Wards and Charms
Throughout history, humanity has turned to wards and charms for protection against unseen forces, particularly during the long, dark nights of winter. In the context of Krampus folklore, these magical and symbolic tools play a central role in safeguarding homes and families from the mischievous and malevolent forces associated with the Yule season. Whether you view them as spiritual safeguards or practical symbols of mindfulness and intention, Yule wards and charms are a powerful way to enhance your defenses. This chapter will guide you through the history, creation, and placement of these protective tools.

1. The Role of Wards and Charms in Yule Traditions

Wards and charms are deeply rooted in ancient Yule traditions, serving as both physical objects and conduits for protective energy. Their use reflects the human need to establish boundaries and invite blessings during the season of darkness and introspection.

- **Wards as Protective Barriers**
  Wards act as invisible shields, creating a boundary that repels negative energies and unwelcome entities, such as Krampus in folklore. They can be physical objects, like sigils or symbols, or intangible protections created through rituals and spells.
- **Charms as Attractors of Positive Energy**
  Charms, on the other hand, are objects imbued with intention to attract positive energies, such as joy, harmony, and abundance. They often carry personal significance and are used to counterbalance the darker forces of the season.
- **Symbolic Significance**
  Many Yule wards and charms are tied to natural elements and ancient symbols, reflecting the season's themes of renewal, light, and protection. Common motifs include evergreen plants, bells, pentagrams, and candles.

2. Essential Tools and Ingredients for Yule Wards and Charms

Creating effective wards and charms requires specific tools and materials, many of which are readily available during the Yule season.

Natural Materials

- **Evergreens (Pine, Fir, Holly, Ivy):** Symbolize eternal life and resilience, often used in wreaths and garlands.
- **Berries (Holly, Juniper):** Represent protection and the cycle of renewal.
- **Salt:** A universal symbol of purification and protection, used to cleanse spaces and create boundaries.

- **Crystals (Quartz, Black Tourmaline, Obsidian):** Amplify protective energy and repel negativity.

Metallic Elements

- **Bells and Chimes:** Their sound is believed to ward off evil spirits and attract benevolent ones.
- **Iron Nails or Horseshoes:** Traditionally used to repel malevolent entities, including Krampus.

Herbs and Spices

- **Cinnamon, Clove, and Nutmeg:** Represent warmth, prosperity, and spiritual protection.
- **Frankincense and Myrrh:** Sacred resins used for cleansing and invoking divine protection.
- **Lavender and Rosemary:** Used to promote peace and dispel negativity.

Symbolic Items

- **Candles:** Represent light overcoming darkness, with white and red being traditional Yule colors.
- **Sigils and Runes:** Custom symbols created to embody specific protective intentions.

3. Creating Yule Wards

Wards are primarily designed to establish boundaries and repel unwanted forces. Here are some effective types of Yule wards you can create:

Wreath Ward

- **Materials Needed:** Evergreen branches, holly berries, a metal frame, red ribbon, and bells.
- **Instructions:**
  1. Arrange evergreen branches in a circular shape on the frame, securing them with twine.
  2. Add holly berries for protection and attach small bells to the wreath to ward off negativity.
  3. Tie a red ribbon around the wreath as a symbol of strength and protection.
  4. Hang the wreath on your front door to shield your home from Krampus and other malevolent forces.

Salt Barrier Ward

- **Purpose: Creates an invisible barrier to block negative energies.**
- **Instructions:**
  1. **Sprinkle a thin line of salt along doorways, windowsills, and other entry points.**
  2. **As you lay the salt, recite a protective incantation, such as:**
     "By the power of the earth and the light of Yule, I cast away all harm and secure this home."
  3. **Replace the salt barrier regularly to maintain its effectiveness.**

Sigil Ward

- **Purpose: Custom-designed symbols for specific intentions.**
- **Instructions:**
  1. **Create a sigil by combining symbols or letters that represent your intention (e.g., protection, harmony).**
  2. **Draw the sigil on parchment, wood, or a stone using red or white ink.**
  3. **Place the sigil near entry points or bury it near your home for long-term protection.**

4. Crafting Yule Charms

Charms are used to attract positive energy and blessings. They are often portable and can be carried or hung around the home.

Protection Sachet

- **Materials Needed: A small pouch, dried herbs (rosemary, lavender, cinnamon), and a protective crystal.**
- **Instructions:**
  1. **Fill the pouch with the dried herbs and a small protective crystal, such as black tourmaline.**
  2. **Tie the pouch closed with red ribbon.**
  3. **Carry the sachet with you or hang it near your bed to ward off negative influences.**

Bell Charm

- **Purpose: The sound of bells is believed to repel Krampus and other malevolent forces.**
- **Instructions:**
  1. **String a small bell onto a red ribbon or cord.**
  2. **Hang the bell on doorknobs or near windows.**
  3. **Whenever the bell rings, visualize it dispelling negativity and calling in positive energy.**

Cinnamon Stick Charm

- **Materials Needed: Cinnamon sticks, twine, and holly sprigs.**
- **Instructions:**
  1. **Bundle three cinnamon sticks together with twine.**
  2. **Add a sprig of holly for extra protection.**
  3. **Hang the charm in your kitchen or living area to invite warmth, prosperity, and protection.**

5. Empowering and Activating Wards and Charms
For wards and charms to be effective, they must be imbued with intention and energy.

- **Ritual Cleansing: Before using any materials, cleanse them with smoke (e.g., sage, palo santo) or saltwater to remove residual energy.**
- **Setting Intentions: Hold the item in your hands and focus on your desired outcome, whether it's protection, harmony, or joy. Speak your intention aloud or visualize it clearly.**
- **Charging with Energy:**
  - **Use moonlight or candlelight to charge the item with protective energy.**
  - **Meditate while holding the item to infuse it with your personal energy.**
- **Recharging Regularly: Wards and charms should be recharged periodically to maintain their effectiveness, particularly during the Yule season.**

6. Placing Wards and Charms Strategically

The placement of wards and charms is as important as their creation. Consider the following locations:

- **Entry Points:** Hang wreaths, bells, or sigils near doors and windows to block entry.
- **Living Spaces:** Place charms in common areas to create a protective atmosphere for the entire household.
- **Bedrooms:** Keep sachets or crystals near the bed to safeguard against nightmares and negative energy.
- **Outdoors:** Bury sigils or protective stones at the corners of your property to create a larger protective boundary.

Conclusion: Crafting a Shield of Light

Yule wards and charms are a beautiful blend of tradition, intention, and creativity. By incorporating these protective tools into your home, you honor ancient customs while creating a safe and harmonious space for your family. Whether you believe in their magical properties or view them as symbols of mindfulness and care, their presence can make your Yule season more joyful and secure. With your home fortified by these powerful tools, you are one step closer to a Krampusproof Yule.

Chapter 7: Protective Yule Altars
Designing an Altar to Invite Positive Energies and Repel Krampus
Introduction: The Power of a Yule Altar

A Yule altar is more than just a decorative centerpiece—it is a spiritual focal point for protection, positivity, and intention during the holiday season. Altars have long been used across cultures as places to honor deities, celebrate the cycles of nature, and shield against negative forces. In the context of Krampusproofing your home, a Yule altar acts as both a beacon of light to invite positive energies and a barrier to repel malevolent influences like Krampus.

This chapter will guide you through the process of designing, constructing, and maintaining a protective Yule altar. Whether you're a seasoned practitioner or new to the idea, you'll learn how to create a sacred space tailored to your needs.

1. The Purpose of a Protective Yule Altar

Before you begin, it's important to understand the key purposes a Yule altar serves:

- **Protection Against Krampus:** Symbolic and magical elements on the altar create a barrier against negative entities, including Krampus.
- **Inviting Positive Energies:** By incorporating seasonal symbols and sacred items, the altar attracts joy, peace, and harmony.
- **Honoring the Spirit of Yule:** The altar becomes a space to celebrate the winter solstice, honor nature, and connect with the spiritual themes of the season.
- **Personal Reflection and Intention Setting:** A Yule altar provides a place to meditate, reflect, and set intentions for the coming year.

2. Choosing a Location for Your Yule Altar

The location of your altar is crucial for its effectiveness and accessibility.

- **Central Placement:** Place the altar in a central location, such as a living room or dining area, to radiate its protective and positive energy throughout the home.
- **Facing Nature:** If possible, position the altar near a window or facing outdoors to connect with the natural cycles of winter.
- **Sacred Corners:** Alternatively, choose a quiet corner of the home where the altar can remain undisturbed, creating a sanctuary-like atmosphere.

3. Essential Components of a Protective Yule Altar

A well-designed Yule altar incorporates elements that symbolize protection, celebration, and the themes of the season. Here are the key components to include:

Seasonal Decorations

- **Evergreens (Pine, Holly, Ivy):** Represent eternal life and resilience, warding off negativity. Arrange them as garlands or small bundles.
- **Candles:** Symbolize the return of the sun and the triumph of light over darkness. Use white (protection), red (strength), and green (renewal) candles.

Symbols of Protection

- **Pentagrams or Runes:** Place protective symbols on the altar to ward off Krampus. These can be drawn on parchment, carved into wood, or cast as charms.
- **Bells:** Their ringing is believed to dispel evil spirits, including Krampus. Arrange small bells on the altar or hang them nearby.
- **Crystals:** Include protective stones such as black tourmaline, obsidian, or clear quartz to amplify the altar's energy.

Sacred Objects

- **Yule Log:** A small decorative Yule log can act as a central symbol of the altar. Adorn it with candles and greenery for added meaning.
- **Incense and Resins:** Burn frankincense, myrrh, or cedar to cleanse the space and create an atmosphere of sacred protection.

Offerings

- **Seasonal Fruits and Nuts:** Apples, oranges, and chestnuts honor the abundance of nature and invite prosperity.
- **Milk and Bread:** Traditional offerings for Yule spirits, symbolizing hospitality and gratitude.

Personal Items

- **Photographs or Keepsakes:** Include items that represent family and loved ones to focus the altar's protective energy on them.
- **Intentions or Wishes:** Write your intentions for the season on paper and place them on the altar to be energized by its presence.

4. Constructing Your Protective Yule Altar

Follow these steps to create an altar that balances beauty, symbolism, and functionality:

Step 1: Cleanse the Space

- Before constructing the altar, cleanse the area with a ritual of your choice, such as burning sage or sprinkling salt water. This removes any lingering negativity and prepares the space for sacred work.

Step 2: Set Up a Foundation

- Use a small table, shelf, or flat surface as the base of your altar. Cover it with a cloth in seasonal colors like red, green, or white.

Step 3: Arrange the Elements

- Place the most prominent symbols, such as the Yule log or a central candle, in the middle of the altar.
- Arrange protective items like pentagrams, crystals, and bells around the perimeter.
- Add seasonal decorations and offerings in a way that feels balanced and visually pleasing.

Step 4: Light the Altar

- Once the altar is complete, light the candles and incense to activate its energy. As you do so, speak an invocation or prayer to focus its purpose, such as:
  "By the light of Yule and the strength of the season, I call forth protection and banish all harm from this home."

5. Maintaining and Enhancing Your Yule Altar

An altar's energy must be maintained and refreshed regularly, especially during the busy Yule season.

- **Daily Rituals:** Light a candle or incense daily to keep the altar active and energized. Use this time for meditation or intention setting.
- **Cleansing:** Periodically cleanse the altar with sage or salt water to remove any accumulated negativity.
- **Rotating Offerings:** Replace perishable offerings like fruits and bread as needed to keep the altar fresh and vibrant.

6. Integrating Family and Tradition

A Yule altar can become a meaningful tradition that involves the whole family. Encourage participation by:

- **Involving Children:** Let children create small decorations or write intentions to place on the altar.
- **Sharing Stories:** Use the altar as a space to tell Yule stories and legends, including those of Krampus and St. Nicholas.
- **Hosting Rituals:** Hold family rituals around the altar, such as lighting candles together or sharing a meal in its presence.

Conclusion: Your Yule Altar as a Beacon of Light

A Yule altar is a powerful tool for transforming your home into a sanctuary of light, love, and protection during the holiday season. By incorporating symbols of the season, protective elements, and personal touches, you create a sacred space that not only repels Krampus but also invites harmony and positivity into your life. As you light your candles and offer your prayers, remember that the altar is a reflection of your intentions and your commitment to a safe, joyful, and meaningful Yule. With your altar in place, you are well on your way to creating a truly Krampusproof home.

Chapter 8: Sacred Herbs and Oils
Using Traditional Plants and Fragrances for Protection
Introduction: The Power of Nature in Protection

For centuries, herbs and oils have been integral to spiritual practices, offering protection, purification, and blessings. During Yule, the darkest time of the year, these natural elements are believed to ward off negativity, repel malevolent entities like Krampus, and invite positive energy into the home. This chapter explores the rich tradition of using sacred herbs and oils for protection during the Yule season, providing practical guidance for incorporating them into your rituals and home.

1. The Historical and Cultural Significance of Herbs and Oils

Herbs and oils hold a special place in Yule traditions due to their symbolic and practical uses.

- **Herbs in Folklore:** Many cultures have attributed protective properties to specific plants, often using them in rituals, wreaths, or charms. For example, evergreen plants like holly and pine have long been associated with resilience and protection against evil.
- **Oils in Spiritual Practices:** Essential oils extracted from sacred plants concentrate their essence, making them powerful tools for anointing, cleansing, and creating protective atmospheres.
- **Winter Symbolism:** The herbs and oils used during Yule often reflect the themes of renewal, light, and safeguarding the home against the challenges of winter.

2. Essential Herbs for Yule Protection
Evergreens: Pine, Fir, and Cedar

- **Symbolism:** Eternal life, resilience, and protection.
- **Uses:**
    - Burn pine or cedar in a fire-safe bowl to cleanse your home.
    - Add sprigs of fir to wreaths, garlands, or charms to create a natural protective barrier.

Holly

- **Symbolism:** Protection, defense, and good fortune.
- **Uses:**
    - Place holly branches near doors and windows to ward off Krampus.
    - Incorporate holly leaves into protective charms or wreaths.

Ivy

- **Symbolism:** Growth, strength, and enduring protection.
- **Uses:**
    - Weave ivy into garlands or use it as an offering on a Yule altar.
    - Hang ivy above doorways to shield the home from negativity.

Rosemary

- **Symbolism:** Purification, clarity, and protection.
- **Uses:**
    - Burn rosemary as incense to cleanse your space.
    - Place sprigs of rosemary in small sachets to carry or hang around the home.

Sage

- **Symbolism:** Cleansing, wisdom, and warding off negative energy.
- **Uses:**
    - Use sage bundles to smudge and cleanse your home of lingering negativity.
    - Sprinkle dried sage around the perimeter of your property for added protection.

Bay Leaves

- **Symbolism:** Victory, protection, and banishment of evil.
- **Uses:**
    - Write protective intentions on bay leaves and burn them in a fire-safe dish.
    - Place bay leaves under your pillow for spiritual protection during sleep.

Juniper

- **Symbolism:** Protection, purification, and dispelling negativity.
- **Uses:**
    - Burn juniper berries or branches to create a protective atmosphere.
    - Incorporate juniper into wreaths or decorative bundles.

3. Essential Oils for Yule Protection

Frankincense

- **Symbolism:** Sacredness, purification, and divine protection.
- **Uses:**
    - Diffuse frankincense oil to cleanse and sanctify your home.
    - Anoint candles or doorways with diluted frankincense oil for added protection.

Myrrh

- **Symbolism:** Spiritual grounding, healing, and banishment of evil.
- **Uses:**
    - Burn myrrh resin or diffuse its oil to create a sacred and protective environment.
    - Mix myrrh oil with a carrier oil to anoint protective charms or objects.

Cedarwood

- **Symbolism:** Strength, purification, and repelling negative energies.
- **Uses:**
    - Diffuse cedarwood oil to fill your home with a protective and grounding aroma.
    - Add a few drops of cedarwood oil to cleaning solutions for an extra layer of cleansing.

Lavender

- **Symbolism:** Peace, purification, and spiritual protection.
- **Uses:**
  - Anoint your wrists or temples with diluted lavender oil for personal protection.
  - Add lavender oil to a spray bottle with water to create a protective mist for your home.

Cinnamon

- **Symbolism:** Warmth, prosperity, and protective energy.
- **Uses:**
  - Diffuse cinnamon oil to create a cozy and energetically secure environment.
  - Anoint candles or wreaths with cinnamon oil for added protective properties.

Peppermint

- **Symbolism:** Cleansing, renewal, and warding off negativity.
- **Uses:**
  - Diffuse peppermint oil for a refreshing and protective aroma.
  - Use peppermint oil in ritual baths for spiritual cleansing and protection.

4. Creating Protective Blends and Ritual Tools

Combining herbs and oils enhances their protective properties. Here are some blends and tools you can create:

Protective Yule Incense

- **Ingredients:** Frankincense resin, myrrh resin, dried rosemary, and cedar shavings.
- **Instructions:**
    1. Grind the ingredients together using a mortar and pestle.
    2. Burn the incense on charcoal in a fire-safe dish during Yule rituals or when you sense negative energy.

Yule Protection Oil

- **Ingredients:** Carrier oil (e.g., jojoba or almond oil), drops of frankincense, cedarwood, and cinnamon oils.
- **Instructions:**
    1. Combine the oils in a small glass bottle.
    2. Use the oil to anoint doorways, windows, or charms for protection.

Herbal Protection Sachets

- **Ingredients:** Dried rosemary, bay leaves, holly berries, and lavender flowers.
- **Instructions:**
    1. Fill small fabric pouches with the herbs.
    2. Hang the sachets around your home or carry them with you for personal protection.

5. Using Herbs and Oils in Yule Rituals

Incorporating sacred herbs and oils into your Yule rituals enhances their potency and meaning.

- **Cleansing the Home:** Use sage or rosemary bundles to smudge your home, starting at the front door and moving clockwise through each room.
- **Anointing Protective Symbols:** Anoint pentagrams, runes, or sigils with protection oil before placing them on your altar or around your home.
- **Blessing the Yule Altar:** Sprinkle dried herbs or burn incense on your altar to create a sacred and protective space.
- **Seasonal Offerings:** Place bundles of herbs or bowls of essential oil blends as offerings on your Yule altar to honor the season and invite blessings.

6. Storing and Maintaining Herbs and Oils

To ensure their effectiveness, herbs and oils must be stored and maintained properly.

- **Storage Tips:**
    - Keep dried herbs in airtight containers away from direct sunlight.
    - Store essential oils in dark glass bottles to preserve their potency.
- **Cleansing Tools:** Periodically cleanse your herb and oil tools (e.g., mortar and pestle, storage jars) to remove residual energy.
- **Refreshing Supplies:** Replace herbs and oils regularly to ensure their vibrancy and effectiveness.

Conclusion: Harnessing Nature's Protective Power

Sacred herbs and oils are invaluable tools for creating a protective and harmonious environment during Yule. By understanding their symbolism, properties, and uses, you can incorporate them into your rituals and home in meaningful ways. Whether you burn rosemary to cleanse the air, diffuse frankincense to ward off negativity, or craft protective sachets to shield your family, these natural elements connect you to ancient traditions and the enduring power of nature. With their help, you can fortify your home and spirit, ensuring that Krampus—and any other dark forces—remain firmly outside your door.

Chapter 9: Building a Krampus-Proof Perimeter
Physical Barriers, Traps, and Security Measures Inspired by Folklore
Introduction: Why a Perimeter Matters

In folklore, Krampus is depicted as a cunning and resourceful figure capable of bypassing traditional defenses. To truly Krampusproof your home, you need to think beyond internal safeguards and focus on building a protective perimeter. A strong, fortified boundary serves as the first line of defense, keeping Krampus—and any other unwelcome forces—at bay. This chapter blends ancient traditions with practical modern techniques, teaching you how to create physical barriers, deploy folklore-inspired traps, and implement security measures that are both effective and symbolic.

1. The Importance of a Perimeter in Folklore

Throughout history, the idea of a protective boundary has been central to warding off evil entities. Krampus folklore emphasizes the need to secure thresholds, such as doors, windows, and property lines, where malevolent forces are believed to enter.

- **Symbolic Significance:** A well-defined perimeter represents the boundary between your safe, sacred space and the chaotic, unpredictable outside world.
- **Folklore Lessons:** Stories often depict Krampus testing physical and symbolic barriers, such as wreaths, charms, or offerings, before gaining entry.

2. Key Areas to Fortify
Property Line

- **Significance in Folklore:** The edge of your property is the first place to mark your territory and set boundaries.
- **Practical Measures:**
    ◦ Install fencing or hedgerows to create a clear boundary.
    ◦ Use natural materials, such as evergreen branches, to blend practical barriers with symbolic protection.

Entryways (Doors and Windows)

- **Significance in Folklore:** Thresholds are liminal spaces where protective energies must be concentrated.
- **Practical Measures:**
    ◦ Reinforce doors with deadbolts and sturdy frames.
    ◦ Install window locks and shatter-resistant glass.
    ◦ Place charms or protective symbols, such as pentagrams or wreaths, at all entry points.

Chimney

- **Significance in Folklore:** In many tales, Krampus enters homes via the chimney, much like Santa Claus.
- **Practical Measures:**
    - Install a chimney cap to block physical entry.
    - Hang bells or wind chimes near the fireplace to detect and repel any supernatural intrusions.

Outdoor Areas (Gardens and Yards)

- **Significance in Folklore:** Open spaces can be used to create deterrents and traps to slow or stop Krampus.
- **Practical Measures:**
    - Keep the area well-lit with motion-activated lights.
    - Use natural barriers, such as thorny plants (e.g., holly or blackberry bushes), to make passage difficult.

3. Folklore-Inspired Barriers
Evergreen Fences and Garlands

- **Symbolism:** Evergreen plants like pine, fir, and cedar symbolize resilience and eternal life, warding off negativity.
- **How to Use:**
    - Line fences, gates, or doorways with evergreen garlands.
    - Create a ring of evergreen branches around the home's perimeter for added protection.

Salt and Ash Circles

- **Symbolism:** Salt and ash have long been used in spiritual practices to create protective boundaries.
- **How to Use:**
    - Sprinkle a line of salt mixed with ashes around your property.
    - Repeat this ritual periodically, especially during *Krampusnacht* (December 5th).

Iron Talismans

- **Symbolism:** In folklore, iron is a potent deterrent against malevolent entities, including Krampus.
- **How to Use:**
    - Hang iron horseshoes or nails above doors and windows.
    - Bury small iron objects along the property line for added protection.

4. Traps Inspired by Folklore
The Bell Trap

- **Folklore Basis:** Bells are believed to repel evil spirits and alert you to their presence.
- **How to Set It:**
    - String small bells along fences, doorways, or even tree branches.
    - If Krampus attempts to enter, the bells will sound, scaring him away and alerting you.

The Birch Barrier

- **Folklore Basis:** Krampus is associated with birch branches, but these can be repurposed as a deterrent.
- **How to Set It:**

   ° Create a barrier of sharpened birch branches around vulnerable areas like chimneys or windows.
   ° Burn a small bundle of birch branches outside as a symbolic warning to Krampus.

The Holly Trap

- **Folklore Basis:** Holly's sharp leaves and bright berries are said to ward off malevolent forces.
- **How to Set It:**
  ° Place holly branches near doorways and windowsills.
  ° Scatter dried holly leaves in areas where Krampus might tread to create a painful physical deterrent.

5. Modern Security Measures for a Krampusproof Home

While folklore-inspired traps and barriers are effective symbols of protection, modern security measures provide additional peace of mind.

Motion-Activated Lights

- **How They Help:** Bright lights startle intruders—human or mythical—and illuminate vulnerable areas.
- **Where to Install:** Place lights near entry points, along fences, and in dark corners of your property.

Surveillance Cameras

- **How They Help:** Cameras act as both a deterrent and a tool for monitoring suspicious activity.
- **Where to Install:** Cover all major entry points, including doors, windows, and the chimney.

Alarms and Sensors

- **How They Help:** Door and window sensors alert you to any unauthorized entry.
- **Where to Install:** Secure all points of access, including basement windows and attic vents.

Security Apps and Automation

- **How They Help:** Smart home technology allows you to monitor and control security systems remotely, adding a layer of convenience and safety.

6. Rituals to Strengthen the Perimeter

Enhance your physical and symbolic defenses with these rituals:

Yule Blessing of the Boundary

- **What You'll Need:** Salt, evergreen sprigs, and a protective incantation.
- **How to Perform:**
  1. Walk the perimeter of your property, sprinkling salt and placing evergreen sprigs at key points.
  2. As you walk, recite a protective incantation, such as:
  "By the power of Yule and the strength of the season, I seal this boundary against all harm."

Firelight Cleansing

- **What You'll Need:** A fire-safe bowl, charcoal, and dried herbs (rosemary, cedar, and juniper).
- **How to Perform:**
  1. Light the herbs on the charcoal and carry the bowl around the perimeter.
  2. Visualize the smoke creating an impenetrable barrier of light and protection.

7. Maintaining Your Krampusproof Perimeter

Building a perimeter is not a one-time task—it requires regular maintenance to ensure its effectiveness.

- **Inspect Physical Barriers:** Check fences, locks, and other security measures for wear and tear.
- **Refresh Symbolic Elements:** Replace salt lines, evergreen garlands, and other natural barriers as needed.
- **Reinforce Rituals:** Perform boundary-blessing rituals periodically to renew their protective energy.

Conclusion: A Shield Against the Darkness

A Krampusproof perimeter is your home's first defense against the forces of darkness, both mythical and real. By blending ancient traditions with modern security techniques, you create a boundary that is both symbolically and practically impenetrable. With your perimeter fortified, you can rest assured that Krampus—and any other threats—will think twice before crossing into your sanctuary. As you continue to build your defenses, remember that protection is as much about intention and vigilance as it is about physical barriers. Let your fortified perimeter stand as a testament to your commitment to a safe and joyful Yule season.

Part III: Active Defense Strategies

Chapter 10: The Bell and the Birch
Utilizing Traditional Tools of Krampus Lore for Defense
Introduction: The Symbolism of Bells and Birch in Krampus Lore

Bells and birch branches are iconic elements in Krampus lore, often depicted in his imagery and integral to his legend. While traditionally used as instruments of discipline and punishment in the hands of Krampus, these tools can also be reinterpreted as powerful symbols of protection. Harnessing their folklore-inspired energy allows you to repel negativity, fortify your home, and ensure that Krampus—and other malevolent forces—stay at bay.

In this chapter, we will explore the historical significance of bells and birch branches, their symbolic meanings, and how to effectively use them as defensive tools in your Krampusproofing efforts.

1. The Historical Significance of Bells in Folklore
Bells as Protectors

- Bells have long been associated with spiritual and physical protection across cultures. Their sound is believed to repel evil spirits, cleanse negative energies, and announce the presence of sacred or protective forces.
- In Krampus lore, bells are depicted as both tools of terror (used by Krampus to announce his arrival) and symbols of protection (used by households to ward off his presence).

Bells in Yule Traditions

- Bells play a central role in Yule celebrations, symbolizing the return of light and the dispelling of darkness. Their clear, resonant tones are said to cut through the gloom of winter, calling in positive energies and banishing malevolent forces.

2. The Historical Significance of Birch in Folklore
Birch as a Symbol of Discipline and Renewal

- In Krampus lore, birch branches are used as instruments of punishment, often depicted as the *ruten* (bundles of birch twigs) Krampus carries to discipline the naughty.
- Beyond their punitive associations, birch trees symbolize renewal, purification, and protection in many pagan traditions. Birch is one of the first trees to regrow after winter, making it a powerful symbol of resilience and cleansing.

Birch in Spiritual Practices

- Birch wood has been used in ritual purification, warding off negative energies, and creating sacred boundaries. Its dual role as a tool for punishment and protection makes it uniquely suited for Krampusproofing rituals.

3. The Protective Power of Bells
Choosing the Right Bells
Not all bells are created equal; selecting the right type is crucial for their protective potency.

- **Materials:** Brass and iron are traditionally associated with protective energy.
- **Size:** Small jingle bells are effective for subtle protections, while larger bells create a commanding presence.
- **Tone:** Look for bells with a clear, resonant tone that feels uplifting and energizing.

How to Use Bells for Defense

- **Hanging Bells at Entry Points:**
    - Hang bells on doorknobs, windows, or gates to create a protective perimeter.
    - Their ringing announces movement and wards off negative energies.
- **Creating a Bell Charm:**
    - String several small bells together with red ribbon (a protective color) and hang them in key areas of your home, such as near the chimney or above the main door.
- **Using Bells in Rituals:**
    - During a Yule ritual, ring a bell to cleanse the space and call in protective energies.
    - Walk the perimeter of your property while ringing a bell to establish a protective boundary.

4. The Protective Power of Birch
Preparing Birch for Protection

- **Harvesting Birch:** If possible, collect birch branches naturally, ensuring you thank the tree and harvest responsibly. Avoid taking too much from one tree to maintain its health.
- **Cleansing Birch:** Cleanse the branches with smoke (sage, cedar, or rosemary) or saltwater to remove any residual energy and prepare them for use.

How to Use Birch for Defense

- **Crafting a Birch Barrier:**
  - Place bundles of birch twigs near doors, windows, and the fireplace to create a symbolic and physical barrier against Krampus.
  - Tie the bundles with red or white ribbon to amplify their protective energy.
- **Creating a Birch Broom:**
  - Construct a small broom from birch twigs to sweep away negative energy from your home's thresholds.
  - Use the broom in cleansing rituals, focusing on areas where energy feels heavy or stagnant.
- **Burning Birch for Cleansing:**
  - Burn small pieces of birch wood in your hearth or a fire-safe container to purify your home and ward off negativity.
  - As the birch burns, recite a protective incantation, such as:
    "With this flame, I cleanse and protect, repelling all harm that may intersect."

5. Combining Bells and Birch for Maximum Protection

Bells and birch branches are even more powerful when used together, blending sound and symbolism to create a comprehensive defense.

Birch and Bell Wreath

- **Materials Needed:** Birch twigs, small brass or iron bells, red ribbon, and evergreen sprigs.
- **Instructions:**
    1. Form a circular base with birch twigs and secure it with twine.
    2. Add evergreen sprigs for additional protective symbolism.
    3. Attach small bells around the wreath, tying them with red ribbon.
    4. Hang the wreath on your front door to repel Krampus and invite positive energy.

Bell-Rung Birch Ritual

- **Purpose:** A ritual to strengthen your home's protective energy.
- **What You'll Need:** A bell, a bundle of birch twigs, and a candle.
- **How to Perform:**
    1. Light the candle and place it in the center of your altar or ritual space.
    2. Hold the birch bundle and walk through your home, sweeping away negative energy from doors, windows, and corners.
    3. Follow with the bell, ringing it to seal the cleansed spaces with protective energy.

6. Folklore-Inspired Defensive Crafts
Krampus-Repelling Birch Wand

- **Materials Needed:** A straight birch branch, red ribbon, and protective runes or symbols.
- **Instructions:**
    1. Sand and smooth the birch branch.
    2. Carve or draw protective symbols, such as runes or sigils, into the wood.
    3. Wrap the handle with red ribbon for added protection.
    4. Use the wand to draw protective boundaries or direct energy during rituals.

Bell and Birch Charm

- **Purpose:** A portable charm for personal protection.
- **Materials Needed:** A small piece of birch wood, a tiny bell, and a leather cord.
- **Instructions:**
    1. Drill a hole in the birch piece to thread the cord through.
    2. Attach the bell to the cord, allowing it to dangle next to the birch.

3. Wear or carry the charm as a personal protective amulet.

7. Maintenance and Recharging
To keep your bells and birch defenses effective, regular maintenance is essential.

- **Cleansing Bells and Birch:** Periodically cleanse your tools with smoke or moonlight to remove accumulated energies.
- **Refreshing Materials:** Replace worn-out birch branches or bells as needed to maintain their strength.
- **Recharging Rituals:** Perform seasonal rituals, such as during the winter solstice, to renew their protective energy.

Conclusion: Harnessing the Power of Tradition
The bell and the birch are more than just elements of Krampus lore—they are potent tools for creating a shield of protection around your home. By incorporating these traditional symbols into your defenses, you honor the wisdom of the past while ensuring a safe and harmonious Yule season. Whether you ring a bell to repel negativity, craft a birch wreath for your door, or combine both in ritual, these practices provide a tangible connection to the protective energies of the season. With the bell and the birch in hand, you are well-equipped to keep Krampus—and all other unwelcome forces—firmly at bay.

Chapter 11: Sacred Symbols and Sigils
Crafting Protective Sigils and Their Proper Placement in the Home
Introduction: The Power of Sacred Symbols

Since ancient times, symbols have been used as tools of protection, manifestation, and connection with higher powers. Whether carved into doorways, drawn on parchment, or painted on walls, sacred symbols act as energetic focal points that shield, empower, and uplift the spaces they inhabit. Sigils, in particular, are personalized symbols crafted with intention, making them one of the most versatile and powerful forms of protection. In this chapter, you'll learn how to create protective sigils and sacred symbols, imbue them with your personal energy, and strategically place them in your home to keep Krampus—and other unwanted forces—at bay.

1. The Role of Symbols and Sigils in Protection

Symbols and sigils work on both a psychological and spiritual level to enhance protection.

- **Psychological Power:** Seeing a sacred symbol in your home can reinforce feelings of safety and remind you of your intentions.
- **Spiritual Power:** Symbols are believed to channel divine or universal energy, creating a protective field that repels negativity.
- **Cultural Relevance:** Many symbols, like the pentagram or protective runes, are deeply rooted in folklore and spiritual traditions, making them particularly effective during Yule.

2. Common Sacred Symbols for Protection
The Pentagram

- **Meaning:** A five-pointed star within a circle, representing balance and protection.
- **Uses:** Place near entry points to create a boundary against malevolent forces.

Runes

- **Examples:**
    ◦ **Algiz (⬦):** Symbolizes protection and defense.
    ◦ **Tiwaz (⬦):** Represents strength and victory.
    ◦ **Eihwaz (⬦):** Associated with resilience and endurance.
- **Uses:** Carve or draw runes on wooden charms, doors, or stones placed around your home.

The Hamsa Hand

- **Meaning:** A palm-shaped symbol representing divine protection and the warding off of evil.
- **Uses:** Hang above doors or in central areas of the home.

The Eye of Horus

- **Meaning:** An ancient Egyptian symbol for protection, health, and safety.
- **Uses:** Place near windows or as part of your Yule altar to guard against malevolent forces.

The Circle

- **Meaning:** A universal symbol of unity and protection, often used in boundary rituals.
- **Uses:** Draw circles around sigils or protective items to enhance their effectiveness.

3. What Are Sigils?

The Definition of a Sigil

A sigil is a custom symbol created to represent a specific intention or goal. Unlike traditional sacred symbols, sigils are unique to the individual who crafts them, making them deeply personal and powerful.

How Sigils Work

- **Focus of Intention:** The act of creating a sigil helps focus your thoughts and energy on a specific purpose, such as protection or banishment.
- **Energetic Anchor:** Once activated, the sigil serves as a spiritual anchor, radiating the energy of your intention throughout your space.

4. Crafting Your Own Protective Sigils

Creating a sigil is a simple but profound process that requires focus and intention.

Step 1: Define Your Intention

- Write a clear and concise statement of your goal, such as:
  - *"My home is protected from all harm."*
  - *"No negative energy may enter this space."*

Step 2: Simplify the Statement

- Remove any repeating letters and vowels, leaving only the unique consonants.
  - Example: *"My home is protected from all harm"* becomes *M H M S P R T C D F L.*

Step 3: Combine the Letters into a Design

- Arrange the remaining letters into a cohesive, abstract design. Feel free to rotate, overlap, or stylize the letters until they no longer resemble the original alphabet.

Step 4: Refine the Symbol

- Continue tweaking the design until it feels complete and visually appealing to you.

Step 5: Charge the Sigil

- Infuse your sigil with energy through meditation, visualization, or ritual. Visualize your intention being absorbed into the sigil as you repeat your protective statement.

5. Activating and Empowering Your Sigils

Once you've created a sigil, it needs to be activated to release its protective energy.

Methods of Activation

- **Fire:** Burn the sigil on a piece of paper, releasing its energy into the universe.
- **Water:** Submerge the sigil in water as part of a cleansing and activation ritual.
- **Meditation:** Hold the sigil in your mind's eye and visualize it glowing with protective energy.
- **Physical Placement:** Place the sigil in a meaningful location and focus on it during a ritual.

Charging with Intent

- To keep your sigil active, recharge it periodically by repeating your intention and visualizing the sigil radiating energy.

6. Strategic Placement of Sigils and Symbols in the Home

Where you place your sigils and symbols significantly impacts their effectiveness.

Entry Points

- **Doors:** Draw or affix a sigil above or near every entrance to prevent negative entities from entering.
- **Windows:** Place sigils on windowpanes or draw them on the frames using chalk or invisible ink.

Living Spaces

- **Central Rooms:** Position protective symbols in living areas to create a safe and harmonious atmosphere.
- **Fireplace or Chimney:** Draw a sigil near the hearth to block Krampus's traditional point of entry.

Bedrooms

- **Headboards or Nightstands:** Place a sigil near your bed to protect against nightmares and promote restful sleep.

Outdoor Spaces

- **Property Line:** Draw or bury sigils along your property line to establish a protective boundary.
- **Garden:** Use natural materials, such as stones or wood, to carve sigils and place them in your garden.

7. Incorporating Sigils into Yule Decorations
Sigil Ornaments

- Paint or carve protective sigils onto Yule ornaments and hang them on your tree or around your home.

Wreaths

- Add carved or painted sigils to your Yule wreath for an extra layer of protection at your front door.

Candles

- Draw sigils onto candles and burn them as part of your Yule rituals.

8. Maintaining and Refreshing Sigils

Sigils can lose their potency over time, especially if placed in high-energy or heavily trafficked areas.

Cleansing Sigils

- Cleanse sigils with smoke (sage, cedar, or lavender) or moonlight to remove residual energy.

Recharging Sigils

- Periodically meditate on your sigil or repeat the activation ritual to renew its energy.

Refreshing Placement

- Replace worn-out or faded sigils with new ones to maintain their protective effectiveness.

Conclusion: Creating a Fortress of Symbolic Protection

Sacred symbols and sigils are invaluable tools for fortifying your home and spirit against Krampus and other negative forces. By thoughtfully crafting and strategically placing these symbols, you can create a powerful shield that radiates protection, harmony, and positivity throughout your space. As you embrace this practice, remember that the true power of symbols and sigils lies in your intention and belief. With their energy infused into your home, you can face the Yule season with confidence and peace of mind, knowing your sanctuary is safe and secure.

Chapter 12: Protective Runes and Talismans
Harnessing Ancient Runic Magic to Repel Negative Entities
Introduction: The Timeless Power of Runes and Talismans

Runes and talismans have been used for centuries as tools of protection, guidance, and empowerment. Rooted in ancient Norse and Germanic traditions, runes are not just symbols but powerful conduits of energy and intent. Combined with talismans—physical objects imbued with protective energies—they create a dual layer of defense that is both mystical and practical. During the Yule season, these ancient tools can serve as a formidable shield against Krampus and other negative entities, safeguarding your home and loved ones.

In this chapter, we'll explore the origins and meanings of protective runes, the art of creating runic talismans, and the best practices for activating and placing them in your home.

1. The Origins and Symbolism of Runes
What Are Runes?

Runes are an ancient alphabet known as the **Elder Futhark**, used by early Germanic peoples for communication, divination, and magical practices. Each rune carries a unique symbolic meaning and energy, making them ideal for protective work.

Runes as Protective Tools

- In folklore, runes were carved on weapons, tools, and buildings to invoke protection and repel harm.
- Protective runes often represent themes of strength, resilience, and divine guardianship.

2. Protective Runes and Their Meanings

Here are some of the most powerful runes for protection and how to use them:

1. Algiz (⟡)

- **Meaning:** Protection, defense, divine connection.
- **Uses:** Place this rune at entry points or wear it as a talisman to invoke spiritual guardianship and repel danger.

2. Thurisaz (⟡)

- **Meaning:** Defensive force, protection against enemies.
- **Uses:** Draw or carve this rune on windows or near thresholds to deter malicious entities.

3. Eihwaz (⟡)

- **Meaning:** Endurance, resilience, defense against harm.
- **Uses:** Incorporate this rune into charms or shields for long-lasting protection.

4. Tiwaz (◈)

- **Meaning:** Strength, victory, divine justice.
- **Uses:** Use this rune to overcome challenges and protect against external threats.

5. Sowilo (◈)

- **Meaning:** Sun, light, invincibility.
- **Uses:** Place this rune on candles or in your home to ward off darkness and negativity.

6. Hagalaz (◈)

- **Meaning:** Disruption, natural protection, cleansing.
- **Uses:** Use this rune to break and repel negative energy from your space.

3. The Role of Talismans in Protection
What Are Talismans?

Talismans are physical objects imbued with intention and energy for a specific purpose. When combined with runes, they become personalized tools for protection.

Why Use Talismans?

- **Physical Representation:** Talismans provide a tangible anchor for your intentions.
- **Amplification of Energy:** They enhance the potency of the runes or symbols carved into them.
- **Portability:** Talismans can be worn, carried, or placed in strategic locations to extend their protective energy.

4. Crafting Protective Runic Talismans
Materials Needed

- A base material for the talisman (wood, stone, metal, or clay).
- A tool for carving or inscribing runes (knife, chisel, or marker).
- Optional: Paint or ink in protective colors (red, black, or white).

Step-by-Step Instructions

1. **Choose the Rune(s):** Select runes that align with your protective intentions (e.g., Algiz for overall protection or Tiwaz for strength).
2. **Prepare the Talisman:** Cleanse the base material by passing it through smoke (sage or cedar) or placing it under moonlight.
3. **Inscribe the Rune:** Carefully carve or draw the chosen rune onto the talisman.

4. **Add Personal Energy:** Hold the talisman in your hands and focus on your intention. Visualize the rune glowing with protective energy.
5. **Seal the Energy:** Use a protective oil (e.g., frankincense or cedar) to anoint the talisman, sealing its energy.

5. Activating and Charging Runes and Talismans

Once created, runes and talismans need to be activated and charged to unlock their full potential.

Activation Ritual

1. **Cleansing:** Smudge the talisman with sage, rosemary, or cedar to remove residual energy.
2. **Invocation:** Hold the talisman and recite an incantation, such as:
   "By the power of Yule and the strength of the runes, I activate this talisman to protect and shield against all harm."
3. **Elemental Charging:** Expose the talisman to the elements (e.g., bury it in earth, pass it through flame, sprinkle it with water, and wave it in the air).

Charging Methods

- **Sunlight or Moonlight:** Place the talisman under natural light to recharge its energy.
- **Crystals:** Surround the talisman with protective crystals (e.g., black tourmaline or clear quartz).
- **Energy Work:** Meditate with the talisman, visualizing it drawing energy from the universe.

6. Placing Runes and Talismans in Your Home

Strategic placement is key to maximizing the protective energy of runes and talismans.

Entry Points

- Carve or affix runic talismans above doorways or windows to block negative entities.
- Draw runes on doors or use chalk to inscribe them on thresholds.

Living Spaces

- Place talismans in common areas to create a harmonious and secure environment.
- Position larger protective symbols, like Algiz, in central locations to radiate energy throughout the home.

Personal Spaces

- Keep a talisman on your bedside table to guard against nightmares or spiritual intrusion.
- Place a runic charm in children's rooms to provide additional protection.

Outdoors

- Bury talismans along the perimeter of your property to establish a protective boundary.
- Hang runic symbols on fences or trees to shield your outdoor spaces.

7. Maintaining and Refreshing Runes and Talismans
Regular Cleansing

- Periodically cleanse talismans with smoke or moonlight to remove built-up energy.

Recharging Rituals

- Repeat the activation ritual at the start of each season or during significant astrological events.

Replacing Talismans

- If a talisman becomes damaged or feels energetically depleted, thank it for its service and replace it with a new one.

8. Combining Runes and Talismans with Other Protective Tools
Enhance the power of runes and talismans by pairing them with complementary protective practices:

- **Sigils:** Combine runes with custom sigils for a personalized protective system.
- **Herbs and Oils:** Place talismans near protective herbs (e.g., rosemary or holly) to amplify their energy.
- **Altars:** Include talismans on your Yule altar to create a focal point for protective rituals.

Conclusion: Unleashing Ancient Protection
Runes and talismans are timeless tools that tap into the wisdom and power of ancient traditions. By crafting and activating these symbols with intention, you can create a personalized defense system that repels negative entities, including Krampus, and shields your home with enduring strength. With runes and talismans placed strategically throughout your space, you not only honor the protective practices of the past but also ensure a safe and harmonious Yule season for you and your loved ones.

Chapter 13: Krampus Traps and Decoys
Setting Distractions and Traps to Redirect Krampus's Attention
Introduction: Outsmarting the Yule Menace

In folklore, Krampus is portrayed as cunning and relentless, making him a formidable opponent. However, like many malevolent entities, he can be misled, distracted, or even trapped. By leveraging the rich traditions and symbolic tools of Yule, you can create Krampus traps and decoys designed to redirect his focus away from your home and loved ones. These measures combine the ingenuity of folklore with practical strategies to ensure a safe and Krampus-free Yule season.

This chapter explores the art of crafting traps and decoys, their placement, and the techniques to outwit Krampus, turning his own mythical traits against him.

1. The Concept of Trapping and Distracting Krampus
Why Traps and Decoys Work

- **Folklore Insights:** Stories suggest that Krampus, despite his terrifying nature, is often tricked or thwarted by cleverness.
- **Distraction as Protection:** Redirecting his attention with decoys or enticing traps can prevent him from targeting your household.

The Psychology of Krampus

- **Driven by Naughty Behavior:** Krampus is drawn to mischief and disorder, making decoys designed to mimic these traits highly effective.
- **Fascination with Chaos:** He is said to be distracted by objects or situations that pique his curiosity or challenge his cunning.

2. Materials for Crafting Krampus Traps

Before setting your traps, gather the materials needed to construct them effectively. These materials are inspired by folklore and practical defensive techniques.

Key Materials

- **Birch Twigs:** A symbol of Krampus's own tools, used to lure or bind him.
- **Chains or Bells:** The sound of clinking chains and ringing bells is believed to repel or confuse Krampus.
- **Evergreen Branches:** Represent resilience and protection, used to disguise traps or create barriers.

- **Red and White Ribbons:** Traditional Yule colors that signify protection and can act as lures.
- **Iron Objects:** Known to repel malevolent entities, iron nails or rods can reinforce traps.
- **Candles and Incense:** Symbolic and practical elements to draw Krampus to specific locations.
- **Offerings:** Food items like apples, nuts, or bread can act as bait in decoys.

3. Designing Krampus Traps

Traps should be designed to either immobilize Krampus or confuse and redirect his focus. Here are some traditional and creative trap ideas:

The Birch Bind Trap

- **Purpose:** Immobilize Krampus temporarily.
- **How to Create:**
    1. Bundle birch twigs into a figure-eight shape and secure them with red ribbon.
    2. Place the trap near an entry point, such as a doorway or window.
    3. Enchant the trap with a binding spell, such as:
       "By this birch and ribbon tight, I bind your steps this Yule night."

The Chain Ring Trap

- **Purpose:** Confuse and disorient Krampus.
- **How to Create:**
    1. Arrange a ring of chains on the ground near a suspected entry point.
    2. Ensure the chains overlap to create a continuous loop, symbolically entrapping him.
    3. Hide the chain ring with evergreen branches to disguise it.

The Bell Barrier

- **Purpose:** Startle and repel Krampus.
- **How to Create:**
    1. Hang strings of small bells near windows, doors, or chimneys.
    2. Attach bells to motion sensors or lightweight tripwires so they jingle when disturbed.
    3. The sudden sound will act as both a warning to you and a deterrent to Krampus.

4. Crafting Effective Decoys

Decoys work by enticing Krampus to focus on them instead of your family or home. These can be symbolic or material distractions.

The Naughty Child Decoy

- **Purpose:** Exploit Krampus's folklore-driven focus on misbehaving children.
- **How to Create:**
  1. Dress a scarecrow or mannequin in ragged clothing to mimic a child's silhouette.
  2. Scatter items around the decoy to suggest mischief, such as broken toys or candy wrappers.
  3. Place the decoy in a visible outdoor location, such as a yard or porch.

The Offering Pile

- **Purpose:** Redirect Krampus with an offering of symbolic value.
- **How to Create:**
  1. Arrange apples, bread, nuts, and coins in a decorative pile on a plate or tray.
  2. Place the offering in an area away from your home, such as a garden or fence line.
  3. Surround the offering with protective herbs like rosemary or sage to ensure Krampus doesn't linger.

The Mischief Trap

- **Purpose:** Distract Krampus by mimicking the chaos he seeks.
- **How to Create:**
  1. Scatter small items, such as jingle bells, toys, or tangled ribbons, in a specific area.
  2. Use motion-activated lights or sound emitters to startle him if he approaches the decoy.

5. Placement of Traps and Decoys
Strategic placement ensures that traps and decoys are effective in diverting Krampus.
Entry Points

- Set traps near doors, windows, chimneys, and any other potential entryways into your home.
- Use decoys to draw Krampus's attention away from these vulnerable areas.

Outdoor Areas

- Place decoys in yards, gardens, or near fences to keep Krampus occupied outside.
- Use traps along pathways or near gates to intercept his approach.

High-Traffic Areas

- Identify areas in your home that are heavily used, such as living rooms or hallways, and position traps nearby to ensure coverage.

6. Activating and Monitoring Traps
Once your traps and decoys are in place, activate them and monitor their effectiveness.
Activation Ritual

- To enhance the potency of your traps, perform a protective ritual:
    1. Light a candle or incense near each trap or decoy.
    2. Recite an incantation to charge the trap with energy, such as:
       "By the light of Yule and the strength of the season, this trap shall hold, this decoy shall deceive."

Monitoring Tools

- Use motion-activated cameras or alarms to keep watch over trap locations.
- Check traps and decoys daily to ensure they remain intact and functional.

7. Enhancing Traps with Symbolic Elements

Incorporating sacred symbols and materials can increase the effectiveness of your traps and decoys.

Protective Symbols

- Paint or carve runes like Algiz or Thurisaz onto traps for added defensive energy.

Herbs and Oils

- Sprinkle protective herbs like salt, rosemary, or cedar around traps.
- Anoint decoys with oils like frankincense or myrrh to enhance their energy.

8. Maintenance and Refreshing

Traps and decoys may lose their potency over time, especially if disturbed by weather or other forces.

Regular Inspections

- Check traps for physical wear and replace damaged elements.

Recharging Rituals

- Reinvigorate traps and decoys with seasonal rituals, such as on the winter solstice or during *Krampusnacht*.

Conclusion: Outsmarting the Shadow of Yule

Krampus traps and decoys are not just folklore-inspired defenses—they are acts of creativity, intention, and strategic thinking. By leveraging the cunning of tradition, you can mislead and deter even the most persistent of threats. As you set your traps and craft your decoys, remember that the process itself is an affirmation of your strength and ingenuity. With these tools in place, you can celebrate the Yule season with confidence, knowing that you've outwitted the shadowy visitor and ensured the safety of your home and loved ones.

Chapter 14: Sound as a Weapon
Using Bells, Chants, and Music to Repel Krampus and Attract Goodwill
Introduction: The Vibrational Power of Sound

Sound has been used across cultures as a powerful tool for protection, healing, and spiritual transformation. In the context of Yule and Krampus lore, sound serves as both a shield against negative forces and a beacon for goodwill. The resonant tones of bells, the harmonics of chants, and the uplifting energy of music can dispel darkness, repel malevolent entities like Krampus, and fill your home with protective vibrations.

This chapter explores the rich history of sound in spiritual traditions and provides practical guidance on using bells, chants, and music as part of your Krampusproofing strategy.

1. The Protective Power of Sound
Sound as a Barrier

- Sound creates vibrational energy that can clear negativity and create a protective shield.
- Certain frequencies are believed to disrupt harmful energies and entities, making sound an effective tool for spiritual defense.

Folklore and Sound

- In many cultures, sound is used to ward off evil spirits. For example:
    - Bells are rung to cleanse spaces and repel malevolent forces.
    - Chants and mantras are recited to invoke divine protection.
    - Festive music is played to uplift the spirit and banish fear.

2. Bells: Tools of Repulsion and Protection
The Role of Bells in Krampus Lore

- In Krampus traditions, bells have a dual association:
    - Krampus uses large, heavy bells to announce his arrival and instill fear.
    - Conversely, small, high-pitched bells are used by households to repel him.

Choosing the Right Bells

- **Material:** Brass and iron are traditional materials associated with protection.
- **Tone:** Higher-pitched bells are more effective for clearing and repelling, while deeper tones create grounding and stabilizing effects.

- **Size:** Small bells can be hung around the home, while larger bells are ideal for ceremonial use.

Using Bells for Protection

- **Hanging Bells:**
  - Place bells on doors, windows, and fireplaces to create a sonic barrier.
  - Every time the bells jingle, they cleanse the space and repel negativity.
- **Bell Ritual:**
  - Walk through your home while ringing a bell, starting at the front door and moving clockwise.
  - Visualize the sound pushing out any negative energy.
  - Focus on entry points like doors, windows, and chimneys.

Creating a Bell Garland

- String small bells onto a red ribbon and hang the garland above doorways or windows.
- This creates a continuous protective vibration every time the bells move.

3. Chants: Invoking Divine Protection
The Power of Spoken Word

- Chants and mantras use the vibrational energy of spoken words to shift the energy of a space.
- Repeated rhythms and harmonics create a meditative state, amplifying the chant's protective intent.

Protective Chants for Yule

- **Traditional Yule Chant:**
  - *"By the light of the sun and the warmth of the fire, I call protection for all I desire."*
  - Repeat this chant three times while focusing on your intention.
- **Krampus Banishing Chant:**
  - *"Darkness fades, shadows fall, no harm shall come to us at all. Krampus flee, leave this place, only light shall fill this space."*
  - Chant this at doorways or near the fireplace.

How to Use Chants

- **During Rituals:** Incorporate chants into protective rituals, such as lighting candles or placing sigils.
- **As a Daily Practice:** Chant during meditation to maintain a protective energy throughout the season.

4. Music: Filling Your Home with Goodwill
The Role of Music in Yule Traditions

- Music is central to Yule celebrations, symbolizing joy, connection, and the triumph of light over darkness.
- Traditional Yule songs and carols often carry protective and uplifting energies.

Choosing Protective Music

- **Instrumental Music:** Sounds of bells, chimes, or string instruments evoke peace and protection.
- **Traditional Yule Songs:** Songs like *"Deck the Halls"* and *"God Rest Ye Merry Gentlemen"* create a festive and protective atmosphere.
- **Drumming or Percussion:** Rhythmic beats can ground energy and clear negativity.

How to Use Music for Protection

- **Daily Playlists:** Create a playlist of Yule music and play it regularly to maintain a positive energy in your home.
- **Live Music:** Gather family or friends to sing traditional songs or play instruments, amplifying the energy with collective intention.

5. Combining Bells, Chants, and Music
For maximum effectiveness, combine these three elements into a cohesive ritual or practice.
The Sonic Cleansing Ritual

1. **Preparation:** Gather bells, a chant, and a piece of protective music.
2. **Begin with Bells:** Ring a bell at the front door and move through your home, focusing on clearing each space.
3. **Chant for Protection:** Pause in central areas and repeat a protective chant while visualizing light filling the space.
4. **Conclude with Music:** Play uplifting Yule music to seal the protective energy and invite goodwill.

Outdoor Sonic Barrier

- Hang bells in trees or along fences.
- Play music or drum outdoors during the evening to extend the protective energy to your property line.

6. Special Techniques for Krampus-Proofing
Motion-Activated Bells

- Attach small bells to motion sensors near entry points.
- The sound will startle Krampus and alert you to potential intrusions.

Drumming Circles

- Drumming circles are a powerful way to create vibrational energy that repels negativity.
- Gather family or friends and drum in a circle while focusing on your intention to protect your home.

Sacred Sound Baths

- Create a sound bath by playing a combination of bells, chimes, and singing bowls.
- This technique is particularly effective for clearing dense or stagnant energy in the home.

7. Maintenance and Renewal
To keep the protective power of sound active, regular maintenance is essential.
Bell Cleansing

- Cleanse bells with saltwater or sage smoke to remove residual energy.
- Recharge them by exposing them to sunlight or moonlight.

Refreshing Chants

- Update your chants with new intentions as the season progresses.
- Encourage family members to participate for a stronger collective energy.

Music Rotation

- Rotate your Yule playlist to keep the energy dynamic and uplifting.
- Incorporate live performances whenever possible for added potency.

Conclusion: The Harmony of Protection and Goodwill
Sound is a uniquely powerful tool in your Krampusproofing arsenal. Bells create sonic barriers, chants amplify protective energy, and music fills your home with warmth and light. By thoughtfully integrating these elements into your Yule practices, you not only repel Krampus but also create a joyous, harmonious atmosphere that invites positivity and goodwill. Let the resonance of your bells,

the rhythm of your chants, and the melodies of your music transform your space into a sanctuary of safety and celebration this Yule season.

Part IV: Securing the Family

Chapter 15: Teaching Children Krampus Safety
Engaging Children in Safety Rituals Without Fear
Introduction: Empowering, Not Scaring

Krampus, with his dark and mischievous nature, may seem like an intimidating figure for children. However, teaching children about Krampus can be an opportunity to share folklore, reinforce positive behavior, and engage them in family traditions. The key is to approach the topic in a way that empowers children rather than instilling fear, turning safety rituals into fun, creative, and meaningful activities.

This chapter provides strategies for teaching children about Krampus in an age-appropriate manner, engaging them in safety rituals, and making the experience enjoyable and educational.

1. Understanding Children's Perspectives
Why Children Might Fear Krampus

- **Imagery in Folklore:** Stories and depictions of Krampus as a fearsome figure can be unsettling.
- **Unknown Concepts:** Younger children may have difficulty distinguishing between myth and reality.

Turning Fear into Empowerment

- Shift the narrative from fear to empowerment by emphasizing that Krampus is a story and that their participation in rituals helps protect the home.
- Frame safety rituals as proactive and magical rather than reactive or defensive.

2. Introducing Krampus in an Age-Appropriate Way
For Younger Children (Ages 4–7)

- **Simplify the Story:** Present Krampus as a playful figure who only visits when there's mischief, but he can't enter protected homes.
- **Focus on Positive Behavior:** Emphasize that kindness, sharing, and helping others keep Krampus away.
- **Storybooks:** Use age-appropriate books or create your own stories where Krampus learns the importance of being good.

For Older Children (Ages 8–12)

- **Share the Folklore:** Explain Krampus's role as part of Yule traditions, highlighting the balance between reward (St. Nicholas) and discipline (Krampus).
- **Encourage Critical Thinking:** Discuss the moral lessons behind the stories and how they relate to behavior.

- **Introduce Rituals:** Involve them in creating protective rituals or crafting items to keep Krampus at bay.

3. Engaging Children in Krampus Safety Rituals
Crafting Protective Items
Turn the creation of protective items into hands-on, creative activities that children can enjoy.

- **Bells and Ribbons:**
    - Let children decorate bells with ribbons and hang them around the house.
    - Explain how the sound of bells keeps Krampus away and fills the home with joy.
- **Wreaths and Garlands:**
    - Create Yule wreaths using evergreens, holly, and red ribbons.
    - Involve children in placing the wreath on the door as a symbol of protection.
- **Sigils and Symbols:**
    - Teach children to draw simple protective symbols, like stars or circles, on paper or with chalk.
    - Place these symbols on windows, doors, or their bedroom walls as "Krampus shields."

Playful Safety Games
Turn Krampus safety into fun games to keep children engaged.

- **The Krampus Chase Game:**
    - Create a role-playing game where one person pretends to be Krampus, and others must "protect" the home using bells, chants, or symbolic actions.
- **Find the Naughty Spots:**
    - Hide "naughty spots" (cards or small items) around the house.
    - Have children find and "cleanse" them using a bell or protective charm.

Storytelling and Songs
Use storytelling and music to make rituals entertaining and memorable.

- **Story Nights:**
    - Tell stories about Krampus and St. Nicholas with a positive twist, where children learn to outsmart or befriend Krampus through kindness.
    - Allow children to add their own ideas to the story, encouraging creativity.
- **Protective Songs:**
    - Teach children simple songs or chants to "keep Krampus away." For example:
    "Jingle, jingle, bells will ring, keeping Krampus from everything!"

4. Establishing Positive Behaviors
The Role of Positive Reinforcement

- Use Krampus stories to reinforce good behavior without shaming or scaring children.
- Celebrate acts of kindness, sharing, and helpfulness as ways to "keep the family safe."

Creating a Yule Behavior Chart

- Create a chart where children earn stars or stickers for good deeds during the Yule season.
- At the end of the season, reward their efforts with a special treat or activity.

5. Teaching Children Protective Rituals
Introduce simple, child-friendly rituals that they can perform with confidence.
The Bell Ringing Ritual

- **What You'll Need:** A bell for each child.
- **How to Perform:**
    1. Teach children to walk through the house, ringing their bell to "chase Krampus away."
    2. Encourage them to say a simple phrase, like: *"This bell rings loud and clear, keeping all the bad things out of here!"*

The Candle Lighting Ritual

- **What You'll Need:** LED candles for younger children, real candles for supervised older children.
- **How to Perform:**
    1. Gather as a family and light the candles together.
    2. Have each child make a wish or set an intention for protection and kindness.

The Door Guard Ritual

- **What You'll Need:** Chalk or ribbon.
- **How to Perform:**
    1. Show children how to draw a symbol (like a star or heart) near doorways.
    2. Explain that this symbol tells Krampus he's not welcome.

6. Using Krampus to Teach Life Lessons

Krampus stories can provide meaningful lessons about behavior, responsibility, and community.

The Value of Kindness

- Use Krampus's focus on naughty behavior as a way to discuss how kindness and generosity benefit everyone.

Actions Have Consequences

- Explain how Krampus represents the consequences of choices, reinforcing the importance of thinking before acting.

Community and Teamwork

- Frame Krampusproofing as a family effort, teaching children the value of working together to create a safe and happy environment.

7. Encouraging Creativity and Expression

Allow children to express their understanding of Krampus through creative activities.

Drawing and Crafts

- Provide art supplies for children to draw their own interpretations of Krampus or St. Nicholas.
- Encourage them to create "friendly Krampus" designs, turning him into a less scary character.

Writing Stories or Poems

- Ask children to write or dictate their own Krampus tales, focusing on how they would keep him away or teach him to be kind.

Making Krampus Decoys

- Help children build a "naughty decoy" to trick Krampus, turning the task into a fun craft project.

8. Creating a Sense of Safety
Ultimately, the goal is to make children feel secure, empowered, and involved.
Reassuring Children

- Remind children that rituals, symbols, and family efforts ensure their safety.
- Emphasize that Krampus is just a story and cannot harm them in real life.

Celebrating Success

- Celebrate the completion of rituals with a special family activity, like baking Yule cookies or watching a festive movie.
- Frame the rituals as a tradition that strengthens the family bond and makes the season magical.

Conclusion: Turning Fear into Fun
Teaching children about Krampus safety doesn't have to be a source of anxiety. By engaging them in creative, interactive rituals and framing the stories positively, you can turn folklore into a fun and empowering tradition. These activities not only protect your home in the context of Krampusproofing but also teach valuable life lessons about kindness, teamwork, and responsibility. With their newfound confidence and involvement, children will look forward to the Yule season, knowing they've played an important role in creating a safe and joyous home.

Chapter 16: Protective Clothing and Accessories
Crafting Krampus-Resistant Garments for Yule Festivities
Introduction: Wearing Your Protection

Clothing and accessories have been used as tools of protection throughout history, often imbued with spiritual or symbolic meanings. In the context of Yule and Krampus folklore, garments and accessories can be more than decorative—they can act as shields against negative energies and malevolent entities. By incorporating protective symbols, materials, and rituals into your clothing, you can craft Krampus-resistant attire that offers both style and safety for the season.

This chapter explores the history of protective clothing, how to design and craft garments that repel Krampus, and how to imbue them with protective energy.

1. The History of Protective Clothing
Ancient Traditions

- Clothing has long been used to protect against physical and spiritual threats:
  - **Viking Amulets:** Norse warriors wore runic amulets and symbols on their garments for protection in battle.
  - **Medieval Garments:** In the Middle Ages, embroidered crosses or sacred symbols were sewn into clothing for spiritual defense.

Symbolic Accessories

- Accessories like talismans, charms, and enchanted jewelry were commonly worn to ward off evil.

Folklore-Inspired Practices

- In Alpine regions, where Krampus folklore originated, protective garb often incorporated bells, red ribbons, and natural materials like evergreen sprigs to repel malevolent forces.

2. Key Materials for Krampus-Resistant Clothing

Certain materials are believed to have inherent protective properties, making them ideal for crafting garments and accessories.

Fabric Choices

- **Wool:** Associated with warmth and protection, wool is a traditional material for winter garments.
- **Linen:** Known for its cleansing and purifying properties, linen makes an excellent lining for protective clothing.
- **Cotton:** Versatile and breathable, cotton can be enhanced with protective symbols.

Decorative Materials

- **Metallic Threads:** Gold or silver thread can be used to embroider protective symbols.
- **Red and White Ribbons:** These traditional Yule colors symbolize strength (red) and purity (white).
- **Evergreens:** Small sprigs of holly, ivy, or cedar can be attached to clothing for added protection.

Accessories

- **Bells:** Small bells sewn onto clothing create sound vibrations that repel Krampus and negative energies.
- **Iron Charms:** Incorporate iron into buttons or jewelry for its folklore-based protective qualities.
- **Crystals:** Sew small protective crystals, like black tourmaline or amethyst, into hidden pockets.

3. Crafting Protective Garments
Step 1: Designing Protective Patterns

- **Runes and Sigils:** Choose protective runes like Algiz (⧇) or custom sigils and plan where to place them on the garment.
- **Placement Ideas:**
  - Draw runes on the inside of cuffs, collars, or hems.
  - Embroider symbols over the heart or along seams for extra defense.

Step 2: Sewing Protective Clothing

1. **Cleanse Materials:** Before starting, cleanse the fabric and sewing tools with sage or saltwater to remove residual energy.
2. **Incorporate Symbols:**
   - Use embroidery or fabric paint to add protective symbols to visible areas.
   - Sew red or white thread into the lining for subtle protection.
3. **Attach Accessories:** Add bells, charms, or evergreen sprigs as finishing touches.

Step 3: Empowering the Garment

- Before wearing, empower the garment with protective energy through meditation or ritual. Visualize it creating a shield around you as you recite a protection incantation, such as: *"This garment shields me from all harm; no darkness may touch, no evil disarm."*

4. Creating Protective Accessories

Accessories are versatile tools for protection and can be worn daily during the Yule season.

Protective Jewelry

- **Amulets and Pendants:** Create or purchase pendants featuring protective runes, pentagrams, or sacred symbols.
- **Crystal Jewelry:** Wear necklaces or bracelets featuring protective stones like obsidian, black tourmaline, or clear quartz.

Belts and Sashes

- Add red or white ribbons to belts or sashes, tying them around your waist to create a symbolic barrier.
- Embroider protective symbols or sew small bells onto the fabric for additional defense.

Scarves and Hats

- Knit or sew scarves and hats using red and white yarn.
- Incorporate evergreen sprigs or small charms into the design.

5. The Role of Colors in Protective Clothing

Color has significant symbolic meaning and can enhance the protective properties of your attire.

Red

- **Symbolism:** Strength, courage, and protection against malevolent forces.
- **How to Use:** Incorporate red ribbons, thread, or fabric into your garments.

White

- **Symbolism:** Purity, clarity, and divine protection.
- **How to Use:** Use white as a base color for clothing or add white embroidery.

Gold and Silver

- **Symbolism:** Divine light, invincibility, and resilience.
- **How to Use:** Embroider garments with gold or silver thread or wear metallic accessories.

6. Activating and Charging Protective Clothing

To maximize the protective power of your garments and accessories, perform an activation ritual.

The Cleansing and Charging Ritual

1. **Cleansing:** Pass the garment through smoke from sage, cedar, or frankincense to cleanse it of negative energy.
2. **Charging:** Place the garment on your Yule altar and surround it with protective crystals and candles.
3. **Incantation:** Recite a protective chant, such as:
   "By the light of Yule and the strength of the season, this garment shall shield and repel all treason."
4. **Wear with Intention:** When putting on the garment, visualize it creating a shield of light around you.

7. Creating Protective Clothing for Children

Involve children in crafting their own protective clothing to make the process fun and engaging.

Simple DIY Projects

- **Decorate Hats or Mittens:** Let children add small bells, ribbons, or symbols to their winter accessories.
- **Personalized Capes:** Create a "Krampusproof" cape by sewing or painting protective symbols onto a child-sized cape.

Turning Clothing Into a Game

- Frame protective clothing as "magic armor" that helps keep Krampus and other spooky figures away.
- Encourage children to wear their garments proudly during Yule festivities.

8. Seasonal Additions to Everyday Clothing

Not all protective garments need to be custom-made. You can adapt everyday clothing with seasonal additions.

Temporary Decorations

- Attach small bells or sprigs of holly to jackets and coats.
- Use safety pins to secure ribbons or charms to clothing.

Yule Accessories

- Wear festive scarves, brooches, or hairpins featuring protective symbols.
- Add seasonal socks or gloves with symbolic designs.

9. Maintaining and Refreshing Protective Garments

Protective clothing requires regular care to ensure it remains effective.

Cleansing

- Wash garments with salt or protective herbs like rosemary or lavender added to the water.
- Smudge garments with smoke from sage or cedar to refresh their energy.

Recharging

- Place garments under the light of the full moon or sun to recharge their energy.
- Repeat activation rituals during the Yule season to maintain their potency.

Conclusion: Wrapping Yourself in Protection

Protective clothing and accessories offer a unique blend of practicality and symbolism, allowing you to wear your defenses with pride during the Yule season. By incorporating protective symbols, materials, and rituals into your garments, you create a physical and spiritual shield against Krampus and other negative influences. Whether it's a bell-adorned scarf, a rune-embroidered sweater, or a charm-laden necklace, your protective attire serves as a reminder of the strength and resilience within you and your family. Celebrate the season with confidence, knowing you're wrapped in layers of style and safety.

Chapter 17: Guarding the Hearth and Home
The Hearth's Role in Defending the Household from Krampus
Introduction: The Hearth as a Protective Symbol

Throughout history, the hearth has been considered the heart of the home—a sacred space of warmth, nourishment, and protection. In Krampus lore, the hearth holds particular significance as both a point of vulnerability and a place of power. While Krampus is often depicted entering homes through chimneys, the hearth can also serve as a powerful barrier against his malevolent intentions. By understanding its symbolic and practical roles, you can transform your hearth into a fortified shield that protects your household during the Yule season.

This chapter explores the historical significance of the hearth, practical steps to secure it, and rituals to enhance its protective energy.

1. The Historical and Symbolic Role of the Hearth
The Hearth in Folklore

- **Sacred Fire:** In many cultures, the hearth fire was considered sacred, representing the family's connection to divine forces.
- **Guardian Spirits:** Hearths were believed to house protective spirits or deities, such as the Roman goddess Vesta or the Norse god Loki (in his positive, fire-associated aspect).
- **Gathering Point:** The hearth was where families gathered for warmth, storytelling, and rituals, making it the symbolic heart of the home.

The Hearth as a Gateway

- In Krampus lore, the hearth is a liminal space—both a source of comfort and a potential point of entry for malevolent forces.

2. Securing the Hearth Against Krampus

Practical measures can reinforce your hearth as a safe and secure part of your home.

Chimney Caps and Grates

- Install a chimney cap to block physical entry.
- Use a decorative metal grate to protect the hearth when not in use, symbolically "sealing" the gateway.

Bell Barriers

- Hang small bells on the hearth grate or near the fireplace opening.
- Bells create vibrations that repel negative energies and alert you to disturbances.

Evergreen Wreaths

- Place a small evergreen wreath or garland on the hearth mantle.
- Evergreens symbolize resilience and protection, creating a barrier against Krampus.

3. Decorating the Hearth for Protection

The hearth is an ideal location for symbolic decorations that enhance its protective energy.

Protective Symbols

- **Runes:** Carve or paint protective runes, such as Algiz (ᛉ) or Thurisaz (ᚦ), onto the hearth-stone or fireplace tools.
- **Sigils:** Create custom sigils for protection and draw them on the hearth using chalk or paint.

Candles

- Place candles on the mantle to symbolize the light of Yule overcoming the darkness.
- Use red and white candles for added protective symbolism.

Seasonal Decor

- Add holly, ivy, or cedar garlands to the hearth for their protective and purifying properties.
- Incorporate red ribbons, which are believed to repel malevolent forces.

4. Rituals to Protect the Hearth

Enhance the hearth's protective energy with simple but powerful rituals.

Hearth Blessing Ritual

1. **Cleanse the Hearth:**
    - Sweep the hearth clean and remove any ash or debris.
    - Smudge the area with sage, cedar, or rosemary to remove negative energy.
2. **Set the Intention:**
    - Light a small fire or candle in the hearth and say:
    "Sacred flame, protect this home, guard all within, where'er we roam. By this fire, no harm shall pass, no darkness shall this threshold trespass."
3. **Seal the Space:**
    - Sprinkle a circle of salt or protective herbs around the hearthstone.

The Yule Log Ceremony

1. Select a log (preferably oak or birch) to represent the Yule log.
2. Carve protective symbols or sigils into the log.
3. Light the log in the hearth during Yule celebrations, symbolizing the triumph of light over darkness.
4. As it burns, recite a protective incantation:
    "This fire burns bright, a shield of light, guarding us through the longest night."
5. Save the ashes to scatter around your property for additional protection.

The Evergreen Hearth Ritual

1. Gather sprigs of holly, cedar, or pine.
2. Place the sprigs in the hearth and light a small fire, allowing the smoke to rise and cleanse the space.
3. Say:
    "From evergreen to ember bright, this hearth is guarded day and night."

5. Maintaining the Hearth's Protective Energy

The hearth's protective energy must be maintained throughout the Yule season.

Regular Cleansing

- Periodically smudge the hearth with sage or cedar to clear stagnant energy.
- Sweep away ashes and debris to ensure the hearth remains a symbol of purity and protection.

Recharging Rituals

- Repeat the hearth blessing ritual weekly to reinforce its protective energy.
- During the full moon, place protective crystals, such as black tourmaline or clear quartz, on the hearth to recharge its energy.

6. Family Involvement in Hearth Protection

The hearth is a communal space, making it an ideal focal point for family traditions.

Involve Children

- Let children help decorate the hearth with seasonal symbols like holly, bells, or candles.
- Teach them simple chants or songs to "bless the fire" together as a family.

Family Rituals

- Hold regular gatherings around the hearth to share stories, express gratitude, and set intentions for protection and harmony.
- Use the hearth as a focal point for Yule celebrations, emphasizing its role as a source of warmth and safety.

7. Symbolic Stories About the Hearth

Stories can help reinforce the significance of the hearth in a way that resonates with all ages.

The Hearth as a Guardian

- Share tales of protective hearth spirits or family ancestors watching over the home from the fire.

Krampus and the Hearth

- Craft a story where the hearth becomes a magical barrier that Krampus cannot cross, emphasizing its protective role.

8. Expanding the Hearth's Protective Role

The protective energy of the hearth can extend to the entire home.

Using Ash for Protection

- Collect ashes from the Yule log or protective fires and scatter them around the property line to create a barrier against malevolent forces.

Hearth-Inspired Charms

- Craft small charms from hearth ashes, evergreen sprigs, and red ribbon. Place these charms around the home for additional protection.

Conclusion: The Hearth as a Shield

The hearth is more than just a fireplace; it is a sacred symbol of warmth, light, and protection. By understanding its historical significance and embracing practical and symbolic rituals, you can transform your hearth into a powerful shield against Krampus and other negative forces. As the heart of the home, the hearth reminds us of the strength and unity within our families, guarding us through the darkest nights of the year. With your hearth fortified, you can celebrate the Yule season with confidence, knowing your home is protected and filled with the warmth of tradition and love.

Chapter 18: Animal Allies and Their Role
Pets and Wild Animals as Protectors During Yule
Introduction: The Protective Nature of Animals

Animals have long been regarded as spiritual guardians, messengers, and allies in folklore and mythology. During the Yule season, their natural instincts and symbolic significance can be harnessed to protect the home and family from malevolent forces like Krampus. From loyal pets to the mysterious behavior of wild animals, understanding their role in Yule traditions can deepen your connection to the natural world and strengthen your home's defenses.

This chapter explores how pets and wild animals contribute to protection during Yule, ways to honor their role, and practical rituals to involve them in your Krampusproofing efforts.

1. The Historical Role of Animals in Folklore
Guardians in Folklore

- **Dogs:** Often depicted as protectors and guardians, dogs are believed to sense and repel evil entities.
- **Cats:** Revered for their mysterious and spiritual nature, cats are thought to ward off negative energies and serve as mediators between the physical and spiritual worlds.
- **Birds:** Birds like ravens, owls, and crows are symbolic messengers and watchers, often warning of approaching danger.

Animals in Yule Traditions

- In Alpine folklore, animals were believed to sense Krampus's presence and alert humans to his approach.
- Domesticated animals, such as sheep or goats, were often included in Yule rituals to bless the home and ensure protection.

2. Pets as Protectors
Dogs: Guardians of the Threshold

- Dogs' heightened senses make them excellent protectors against physical and spiritual threats.
- Many traditions believe dogs can sense malevolent entities, including Krampus, before humans can.

How to Involve Dogs:

- Place a protective charm on your dog's collar, such as a small bell or a red ribbon.
- Include your dog in family rituals by having them sit near the hearth or threshold during ceremonies.

Cats: Spiritual Shields

- Cats are known for their keen intuition and ability to detect subtle energy shifts.
- Their presence in a home is said to block negative entities from entering.

How to Involve Cats:

- Allow your cat to roam freely, particularly near windows, doors, or the hearth, where their protective energy is strongest.
- Place a cozy blanket or cushion near the hearth or altar to encourage your cat to rest in these areas, creating a natural energy shield.

Other Pets

- **Birds:** Birds in the home, such as parakeets or canaries, can act as vibrational protectors. Their songs and movements raise the home's energy, deterring negativity.
- **Small Mammals (e.g., rabbits, guinea pigs):** While less traditional, these animals are believed to bring calming energy and ground spiritual practices.

3. Honoring Wild Animals During Yule

Wild animals play a significant role in Yule folklore, symbolizing nature's enduring strength and resilience during winter. Their behavior can offer clues about spiritual or environmental changes.

Birds

- **Crows and Ravens:** These birds are often seen as watchers or messengers, warning of danger.
- **Owls:** Associated with wisdom and mystery, owls are believed to protect against unseen threats.
- **Sparrows and Robins:** Their presence near the home is considered a sign of blessings and protection during winter.

Deer and Stags

- Representing gentleness and strength, deer are associated with the spirit of Yule and are believed to ward off evil.
- A stag's antlers, symbolizing defense and protection, are powerful motifs in Yule rituals.

Foxes and Wolves

- These cunning animals are seen as guardians of the wild and protectors of sacred spaces.
- Their tracks near your home during winter can symbolize a spiritual boundary.

4. Creating a Protective Bond with Animals
Strengthening your connection to pets and wild animals can enhance their protective influence.
Daily Interaction

- Spend quality time with pets, reinforcing their role as part of the family's protective circle.
- Feed wild animals responsibly, such as providing birdseed or leaving out scraps for foxes, to foster goodwill and connection.

Animal Blessing Ritual

1. Gather your family and pets near the hearth or altar.
2. Light a candle and place protective herbs like rosemary or sage nearby.
3. Gently touch each animal, saying:
   "By the warmth of this fire and the light of Yule, you are blessed and protected as our guardian true."

5. Involving Animals in Protective Rituals
Bell and Collar Charm

- Attach a small bell or charm engraved with a protective symbol (e.g., Algiz or a pentagram) to your pet's collar.
- The sound of the bell acts as a barrier against negative entities.

Wild Animal Offerings

- Create a natural offering altar in your yard with seeds, nuts, and berries for wild animals.
- Say a blessing to honor their role as guardians of the natural world:
   "To the creatures of winter, guardians unseen, I offer this gift as thanks for your keen protection and grace through this Yule season."

Animal Tracks Ritual

- If you notice wild animal tracks near your home, use them in a ritual:
   1. Trace the tracks with your finger or a small branch.
   2. Say:
      "Guardians of the wild, I honor your path; protect this home from harm's wrath."

6. Creating Protective Spaces for Animals

Ensure that your home and outdoor areas are inviting and safe for animal allies.

For Pets

- Designate a cozy space for pets near the hearth or altar.
- Add protective symbols, such as a red or white blanket embroidered with runes.

For Wild Animals

- Set up bird feeders or shelters to encourage wildlife near your home.
- Plant evergreens or holly bushes to provide natural habitats and additional protective energy.

7. Recognizing Animal Warnings

Animals often sense and respond to danger before humans. Pay attention to their behavior for signs of approaching negativity.

Common Warning Signs

- **Unusual Barking or Growling:** Dogs may alert you to unseen forces near the home.
- **Restlessness or Staring:** Cats may stare at specific areas or act restless when negative energy is present.
- **Sudden Silence or Flight:** Wild birds or animals fleeing an area may signal an approaching disturbance.

8. Honoring Animal Allies in Folklore and Myth

Share stories with your family about the protective roles of animals in mythology to deepen appreciation for their presence.

Mythical Animal Guardians

- **Fenrir's Balance:** In Norse mythology, wolves like Fenrir embody the balance of power and protection.
- **The Stag of Yule:** In Celtic tradition, the stag is a symbol of the winter solstice and a protector of sacred spaces.
- **Cats in Norse Mythology:** Freyja's chariot, pulled by cats, highlights their role as divine protectors.

9. Seasonal Treats and Offerings for Animals
Show gratitude to your animal allies by including them in Yule festivities.
Pet Treats

- Bake pet-friendly Yule cookies using safe ingredients like oats, pumpkin, or peanut butter.

Wildlife Offerings

- Leave out seasonal treats, such as apples, carrots, or unsalted nuts, for deer, squirrels, or birds.

Conclusion: Partners in Protection
Animals, both domesticated and wild, are more than companions during the Yule season—they are vital allies in protecting the home and family. Their natural instincts, spiritual significance, and active participation in rituals create a harmonious connection between humanity and nature. By honoring and involving your animal allies, you strengthen the protective shield around your home and embrace the spirit of Yule. Celebrate their role with gratitude, knowing they stand watch against the darkness and ensure a season of warmth, safety, and joy.

Part V: Fortifying the Spirit

Chapter 19: Invoking Protective Spirits and Deities
Engaging Higher Powers to Shield Your Family
Introduction: Turning to Higher Powers for Protection

For centuries, people have called upon spirits and deities to protect their homes, families, and communities during challenging times. During the Yule season, the darkness of winter and the myths surrounding Krampus make it a particularly meaningful time to invoke these higher powers. Protective spirits and deities provide spiritual strength and guidance, helping to repel malevolent forces and foster harmony within the household.

This chapter explores the spiritual practices, rituals, and invocations that can help you connect with protective entities during Yule. Whether you follow a specific tradition or take an eclectic approach, these methods can provide powerful defenses for your home.

1. Understanding Protective Spirits and Deities
What Are Protective Spirits and Deities?

- **Spirits:** Non-physical entities believed to act as guardians or intermediaries between the human and spiritual realms. These may include ancestral spirits, nature spirits, or household guardians.
- **Deities:** Higher powers worshipped across cultures for their protective, nurturing, or combative qualities. Deities are often associated with specific aspects of life, such as the hearth, family, or nature.

Their Role in Yule Traditions

- **Spirits:** In Yule folklore, household spirits were thought to guard against misfortune and malevolent entities like Krampus.
- **Deities:** Deities associated with light, fire, and the natural cycle of seasons were invoked during Yule to ensure the return of the sun and protection through winter's challenges.

2. Key Deities for Protection During Yule
Norse Pantheon

- **Thor:**
  - **Domain:** Strength, protection, and thunder.
  - **Invocation:** Call upon Thor to defend against malevolent forces and bring courage to your household. Use a hammer symbol, such as Mjölnir, in rituals.
- **Freyja:**
  - **Domain:** Love, protection, and the hearth.
  - **Invocation:** Light candles and offer fragrant herbs like lavender to honor Freyja's protective and nurturing energy.

Celtic Pantheon

- **Brigid:**
    - **Domain:** The hearth, home, and healing.
    - **Invocation:** Place a small bowl of water on your altar as an offering, and light a white candle to invite her blessings.
- **Cernunnos:**
    - **Domain:** Nature, animals, and boundaries.
    - **Invocation:** Use evergreen branches and antler-shaped symbols to honor his role as a guardian of wild spaces.

Greek and Roman Pantheon

- **Hestia (Greek) / Vesta (Roman):**
    - **Domain:** The hearth, domestic harmony, and protection.
    - **Invocation:** Keep a candle or hearth fire burning during rituals to honor her presence.
- **Apollo:**
    - **Domain:** Light, healing, and protection.
    - **Invocation:** Use solar symbols, such as sun-shaped ornaments or gold decorations, to connect with his energy.

Slavic Pantheon

- **Domovoi:**
    - **Domain:** Household spirits and protectors.
    - **Invocation:** Leave small offerings of bread or milk near the hearth to honor and invite the Domovoi's blessings.

Other Traditions

- **Archangel Michael (Christian Tradition):**
    - Known for his role as a protector and leader of heavenly armies, he is often invoked for strength and defense. Light a blue or white candle and recite a prayer for his intercession.

3. Connecting with Ancestral Spirits
The Role of Ancestors

- Ancestors are thought to have a vested interest in protecting their descendants, making them powerful allies during Yule.

How to Honor Ancestral Spirits

- **Create an Ancestral Altar:** Include photographs, heirlooms, or objects associated with your family's heritage.
- **Offerings:** Provide small gifts like food, wine, or seasonal treats to honor their presence.
- **Invocation:** Speak their names aloud during rituals, expressing gratitude for their guidance and protection.

4. Rituals to Invoke Protective Spirits and Deities
Preparation for Rituals

- **Cleanse the Space:** Use sage, cedar, or incense to clear negative energy.
- **Create an Altar:** Dedicate a small space with symbols, candles, and offerings that align with the spirit or deity you wish to invoke.
- **Set Intentions:** Clearly define your purpose, whether it's to protect your family, repel negativity, or foster harmony.

Simple Invocation Ritual

1. **Light a Candle:** Choose a color that corresponds to the spirit or deity (e.g., red for Thor, white for Hestia).
2. **Offer Words of Invitation:**
    - Example:
      "Thor, guardian of strength and protection, I call upon your might to shield my home and loved ones during this Yule season."
3. **Make an Offering:** Present herbs, food, or symbolic items that resonate with the deity or spirit.
4. **Express Gratitude:** Thank the entity for their presence and assistance.

5. Symbols and Tools for Invocations
Sacred Symbols

- **Runes:** Use protective runes like Algiz (ᛉ) or Thurisaz (ᚦ) in your rituals.
- **Sigils:** Craft a personalized sigil representing your intent to invoke protection.

Ritual Tools

- **Candles:** Represent light and divine presence. Choose colors that correspond to the entity you're invoking.
- **Crystals:** Incorporate stones like black tourmaline (protection) or clear quartz (amplification).
- **Sacred Herbs:** Burn or offer rosemary, cedar, or frankincense during rituals.

6. Daily Practices to Maintain Spiritual Protection
Morning Offerings

- Start each day by lighting a candle or incense and offering a brief prayer or gratitude to your chosen deity or spirit.

Household Blessings

- Sprinkle salt or protective herbs around your home's perimeter while invoking the deity's protection.

Sacred Space Maintenance

- Keep your altar or hearth clean and refreshed with new offerings or symbols as the Yule season progresses.

7. Signs of Connection and Protection
Recognizing Signs

- **Dreams:** Visions or symbols in dreams may indicate the presence of a protective spirit or deity.
- **Animal Behavior:** Pets acting unusually calm or protective can signal spiritual support.
- **Energy Shifts:** A sudden sense of peace or warmth often indicates a protective presence.

8. Honoring and Thanking Protective Entities
Expressing Gratitude

- Always thank spirits and deities after rituals, even if their influence isn't immediately visible.
- Offerings of seasonal treats, wine, or handmade crafts are thoughtful ways to show appreciation.

End-of-Season Ritual

- At the close of Yule, perform a gratitude ceremony to honor the protective forces that watched over your family.
- Extinguish candles or fires with a blessing, such as:
  "As this season's light dims, I thank those who protected and guided us. Your presence is honored, your blessings cherished."

Conclusion: Embracing Spiritual Allies

Invoking protective spirits and deities during Yule is a powerful way to safeguard your home and family while deepening your connection to ancient traditions. Whether through ancestral reverence, the invocation of deities, or the guidance of household spirits, these higher powers offer strength, wisdom, and protection. By honoring their presence and maintaining regular rituals, you create a harmonious and fortified space where the light of Yule can shine brightly, free from fear or harm.

Chapter 20: Banishing Rituals for the Yule Season
   How to Banish Negative Energies, Including Krampus, from Your Space
   Introduction: The Importance of Banishing Rituals

The Yule season, with its long nights and rich folklore, is a time when the boundary between light and dark feels particularly thin. While it is a season of joy and renewal, it is also a time to guard against negative energies, including the malevolent presence of Krampus. Banishing rituals are essential practices for clearing unwanted energies, fortifying your home's defenses, and ensuring a peaceful, harmonious environment for your family during the holidays.

This chapter provides a comprehensive guide to banishing rituals, from their historical roots to practical steps you can take to cleanse and protect your space.

1. The Purpose of Banishing Rituals
Why Banishing Is Necessary

- **Clearing Stagnant Energy:** Negative energy can accumulate during stressful times, disrupting the harmony of your home.
- **Repelling Malevolent Entities:** Folklore warns of Krampus and other dark spirits roaming during the Yule season; banishing rituals help repel them.
- **Renewing Protective Boundaries:** Banishing clears old energies and reinforces protective barriers.

Spiritual and Psychological Benefits

- Creates a sense of safety and control.
- Invites positive energy and blessings into your home.

2. Tools and Materials for Banishing
Essential Tools

- **Candles:** White for purification, black for banishing negativity.
- **Herbs:** Sage, cedar, rosemary, or frankincense for cleansing.
- **Salt:** A universal purifier, used to create protective barriers.
- **Crystals:** Black tourmaline, obsidian, or clear quartz for grounding and amplification.
- **Incense or Smoke Sticks:** To cleanse and purify the space.
- **Bells or Chimes:** Sound vibrations to disperse negative energy.

Optional Additions

- **Athame (Ritual Knife):** For directing energy or symbolically cutting away negativity.
- **Sigils or Symbols:** Personalized symbols for banishing and protection.

3. Preparing for a Banishing Ritual
Cleansing the Space

- Start by physically cleaning your home to remove clutter and debris.
- Sweep the floors while visualizing the removal of negativity.

Creating an Altar or Ritual Space

- Dedicate a small area with candles, crystals, and symbols that represent protection and purification.

Setting Intentions

- Clearly define your purpose for the ritual, such as:
    - *"I banish all negativity from this space."*
    - *"No harm or dark force may enter my home."*

4. Step-by-Step Banishing Rituals
The Simple Banishing Ritual

1. **Light a Candle:** Choose a white or black candle and place it in the center of your ritual space.
2. **Burn Cleansing Herbs:** Light sage, cedar, or rosemary and carry it through each room while saying:
   "I cleanse this space of all negativity. Only light and peace may remain."
3. **Ring a Bell:** Use a bell or chime in every corner of the room to break up stagnant energy.
4. **Seal with Salt:** Sprinkle salt along windowsills, doorways, and thresholds, visualizing a protective barrier.
5. **Extinguish the Candle:** Conclude the ritual by thanking any spirits or energies you invoked for assistance.

The Fire Banishing Ritual

1. **Gather Materials:** A fire-safe bowl, a piece of paper, and a black candle.
2. **Write Down Negativity:** Write anything you want to banish—stress, fear, or malevolent entities like Krampus—on the paper.
3. **Light the Candle:** Focus on its flame as a source of purification.
4. **Burn the Paper:** Place the paper in the bowl and let it burn completely, saying:
   "By this fire, I release all harm. Let it return to the void, leaving my space free of darkness."

The Circle of Protection Banishing

1. **Draw a Circle:** Use chalk, salt, or flower petals to create a circle in a central area of your home.
2. **Invoke Protective Energy:** Stand in the circle and call upon a protective deity, spirit, or energy.
3. **Recite a Banishing Chant:**
   "No shadow may cross this line; no harm shall dwell within. By the power of light and love, I banish all that is dark and dim."
4. **Close the Circle:** Sweep the circle away while visualizing any lingering negativity leaving with it.

5. Banishing Krampus: Folklore-Specific Practices
The Bell Barrier Ritual

1. **Gather Small Bells:** Place bells on red ribbons and hang them at all entry points, such as doors and windows.
2. **Ring the Bells:** Walk through your home ringing a larger bell while saying:
   "Krampus, be gone! You have no power here. This home is blessed, and only joy may enter."
3. **Leave the Bells in Place:** Allow the hanging bells to serve as ongoing protection.

The Birch Wand Banishing

1. **Create a Birch Wand:** Use a bundle of birch twigs tied with red ribbon.
2. **Sweep Negative Energy:** Walk through your home, sweeping the air with the wand as if clearing away darkness.
3. **Recite an Incantation:**
   "With birch and firelight, I sweep away the dark. No Krampus shall cross this sacred mark."

6. Maintaining Banished Energy
Daily Practices

- Burn protective incense, such as frankincense or myrrh, each morning.
- Light a white candle in the evening to refresh the home's protective energy.

Seasonal Refreshing

- Perform a banishing ritual at key points during the Yule season, such as the winter solstice or New Year's Eve.

Protective Symbols

- Draw sigils or place talismans around the home to reinforce your defenses.

7. Signs of a Successful Banishing
Energetic Shifts

- The space feels lighter, calmer, and more peaceful.
- Stagnant areas of the home feel revitalized.

Behavioral Changes

- Family members and pets seem more relaxed and harmonious.
- You notice fewer disruptions or unexplained occurrences.

8. What to Do If Negativity Returns
Reassess the Space

- Check for areas where clutter or neglect may have allowed negativity to accumulate.
- Refresh protective barriers, such as salt lines or talismans.

Repeat Banishing Rituals

- Perform a more focused or intensive banishing ritual, incorporating new tools or techniques.

Seek Additional Help

- Call upon a trusted spiritual advisor or practitioner if persistent negativity remains.

Conclusion: Embracing the Light

Banishing rituals are powerful tools for creating a sanctuary of peace and protection during the Yule season. By regularly cleansing your space, invoking higher energies, and reinforcing boundaries, you ensure that your home remains free from negativity and malevolent entities like Krampus. These practices not only shield your household but also invite light, joy, and harmony into your life, aligning with the true spirit of Yule. Let these rituals guide you in transforming your home into a fortress of warmth and positivity, where only love and light may dwell.

Chapter 21: Yule Blessings for Peace and Prosperity
Infusing Your Home with Positive Energy to Prevent Krampus Encounters
Introduction: The Power of Positive Energy During Yule

The Yule season, celebrated during the darkest time of the year, is a powerful opportunity to bring light, peace, and prosperity into your home. By filling your space with positive energy, you not only create a harmonious environment but also prevent malevolent forces, including Krampus, from finding a foothold. Yule blessings are rituals and practices designed to attract abundance, strengthen family bonds, and maintain spiritual balance, making them an essential part of your Krampusproofing strategy.

This chapter explores the importance of Yule blessings, how to perform them, and ways to infuse every corner of your home with light and joy.

1. The Role of Blessings in Yule Traditions
Historical Significance

- **Ancient Practices:** In many cultures, Yule blessings were performed to mark the return of the sun, symbolizing renewal and abundance.
- **Household Protection:** Blessings were used to safeguard families and ensure a bountiful year ahead.

Why Blessings Prevent Krampus

- **Positive Energy as a Shield:** High vibrational energy repels dark entities like Krampus, who thrive in negativity.
- **Fortifying Spiritual Boundaries:** Blessings reinforce protective barriers, making your home inhospitable to malevolent forces.

2. Preparing for a Yule Blessing
Cleansing the Space

- Before performing a blessing, cleanse your home to remove lingering negative energy.
- Use sage, cedar, or rosemary to smudge each room, focusing on corners, entryways, and the hearth.

Setting Intentions

- Decide what you want to achieve with your blessing, such as peace, prosperity, or protection.
- Write down your intentions on paper to focus your energy during the ritual.

Gathering Materials

- **Candles:** White for purity, gold or green for prosperity, and red for strength.
- **Herbs:** Bay leaves, cinnamon, or holly for abundance and protection.
- **Crystals:** Clear quartz for amplification, citrine for prosperity, and amethyst for harmony.
- **Offerings:** Seasonal treats, such as bread, fruit, or wine, to honor spiritual forces.

3. Performing a Yule Blessing Ritual
Step 1: Create a Sacred Space

1. Select a central location in your home, such as near the hearth or Yule altar.
2. Arrange candles, crystals, and offerings in a circle or on the altar.

Step 2: Light the Candles

1. Begin by lighting the candles, starting with the white candle for purification.
2. As each candle is lit, recite an intention:
    - *"With this flame, I call forth peace."*
    - *"With this flame, I invite prosperity."*
    - *"With this flame, I strengthen protection."*

Step 3: Bless the Space

1. Walk through your home with a lit candle or incense, reciting a blessing:
   "By the light of Yule and the warmth of this season, I bless this home with peace and joy, prosperity unending, and love everlasting."
2. Visualize light filling each room and pushing out any residual darkness.

Step 4: Seal the Blessing

1. Sprinkle salt or protective herbs, such as cinnamon or bay leaves, along windowsills and doorways.
2. Say:
   "This home is sacred, this space is blessed. No harm may enter, no darkness oppress."

4. Yule Symbols for Peace and Prosperity

Incorporate symbolic decorations and items to enhance the blessing's energy.

Evergreens

- **Symbolism:** Resilience, renewal, and eternal life.
- **How to Use:** Place evergreen garlands or wreaths around the home to attract prosperity and guard against negativity.

Candles

- **Symbolism:** The return of the sun and the triumph of light over darkness.
- **How to Use:** Arrange candles in a spiral or circle to symbolize unity and abundance.

Holly and Ivy

- **Symbolism:** Protection and the intertwining of peace and growth.
- **How to Use:** Place sprigs of holly and ivy on the mantle, near entryways, or on your altar.

Sun Symbols

- **Symbolism:** Vitality, joy, and prosperity.
- **How to Use:** Add sun-shaped ornaments to your Yule tree or hang them near windows.

5. Blessing Specific Areas of the Home

The Hearth

- **Why It Matters:** The hearth is the heart of the home, representing warmth, family, and protection.
- **Blessing Ritual:**
    - Light a small fire or candle in the hearth.
    - Sprinkle cinnamon or dried orange peels into the flame while saying:
      "This hearth burns bright, a beacon of peace and light."

Entryways

- **Why They Matter:** Doors and windows are symbolic thresholds that must be guarded.
- **Blessing Ritual:**
    - Mark doorways with chalk or draw protective symbols using saltwater.
    - Say:
      "No shadow may cross, no harm may pass; this threshold is blessed with light that lasts."

Bedrooms

- **Why They Matter:** Bedrooms are places of rest and renewal, requiring harmony and peace.
- **Blessing Ritual:**
    - Place amethyst or clear quartz under pillows.
    - Light a small white candle and recite:
    "This space is safe, this rest is blessed, may peace and dreams bring us their best."

6. Inviting Prosperity into Your Home
Creating a Prosperity Jar

1. Fill a small jar with coins, cinnamon sticks, bay leaves, and cloves.
2. Place the jar near your Yule altar or in a prominent area.
3. Shake the jar daily while saying:
   "Abundance flow, prosperity grow, by the light of Yule, may blessings show."

The Blessing Table

1. Arrange seasonal foods like bread, apples, nuts, and wine on a table.
2. Share a meal with your family, dedicating the feast to peace and prosperity.

Using Crystals

- Place citrine or pyrite near windows or on your altar to attract wealth and success.

7. Daily Practices for Maintaining Positive Energy
Morning Ritual

- Light a candle and recite a short affirmation, such as:
  "Peace fills this home, prosperity abounds, and love surrounds us."

Evening Gratitude Practice

- Gather as a family to share something you're grateful for, reinforcing positive energy in the home.

Seasonal Maintenance

- Repeat the Yule blessing ritual at key points during the season, such as the winter solstice or New Year's Day, to refresh the energy.

8. Recognizing the Effects of Yule Blessings
Signs of Peace and Prosperity

- A calmer, more harmonious atmosphere in the home.
- Increased opportunities, such as financial gains or strengthened relationships.
- A sense of spiritual balance and protection.

Conclusion: Filling Your Home with Light

Yule blessings are a powerful way to transform your home into a sanctuary of peace, prosperity, and protection. By performing these rituals with intention and care, you align yourself with the positive energies of the season, ensuring that malevolent forces like Krampus have no place in your space. Through light, love, and abundance, you create a harmonious environment where your family can thrive and celebrate the true spirit of Yule. Let these blessings guide you as you embrace the joy and renewal of the season, confident in the warmth and safety of your home.

Chapter 22: Incorporating Krampus Lore into Safe Traditions
Honoring the Myth Without Inviting the Danger
Introduction: Embracing the Legend Safely

Krampus, the horned and fearsome figure of Alpine folklore, has captivated imaginations for centuries. While his role as a punisher of misdeeds may seem dark, Krampus can also be viewed as a symbol of balance and the importance of accountability during the Yule season. Incorporating Krampus lore into your holiday traditions can be a fun and meaningful way to honor the legend while ensuring that the energy remains positive and protective.

This chapter explores ways to celebrate and incorporate Krampus into your Yule festivities in a safe and empowering manner, turning the darker aspects of his mythology into opportunities for storytelling, learning, and creative expression.

1. The Role of Krampus in Yule Folklore
A Balancing Force

- In folklore, Krampus represents the balance of light and dark, working alongside St. Nicholas to reward good behavior and punish the naughty.
- His presence serves as a reminder of personal responsibility and the consequences of our actions.

Krampus as a Symbol

- Beyond punishment, Krampus symbolizes transformation, encouraging us to confront and release negativity before entering the light of a new year.

Why Incorporate Krampus into Traditions?

- To honor Alpine folklore and its rich cultural heritage.
- To use his story as a teaching tool for children about the value of kindness and accountability.

2. Creating a Safe Space for Krampus Lore
Setting Boundaries

- Clearly establish that your traditions honor the myth of Krampus without inviting his darker energies into your home.
- Use positive intentions and protective rituals to create a safe space for celebrating the lore.

Protective Preparations

- Perform a house blessing before starting any Krampus-themed activities to ensure your space is shielded.
- Use symbols of protection, such as runes or sigils, in decorations and rituals.

3. Storytelling and Education
Age-Appropriate Storytelling

- For young children, present Krampus as a mischievous figure who learns the importance of kindness and cooperation.
- For older children and adults, explore the duality of Krampus and St. Nicholas as symbols of reward and consequence.

Creating Your Own Stories

- Rewrite Krampus tales with positive twists, such as him helping families overcome challenges or rewarding those who change their ways.
- Involve family members in crafting the story, turning it into a collaborative tradition.

Books and Films

- Share Krampus-inspired books or films that highlight the folklore in fun or creative ways, ensuring the content is family-friendly.

4. Krampus-Inspired Crafts and Decorations
Crafting Safe Krampus Icons

- **Krampus Dolls or Figurines:** Create small, playful versions of Krampus using clay, fabric, or paper.
- **Ornaments:** Make Krampus-themed ornaments for your Yule tree, using red and black designs to represent his traditional colors.

Decorative Wreaths

- Incorporate elements of Krampus lore, such as bells, birch twigs, and red ribbons, into a wreath.
- Add protective symbols, like pentagrams or evergreen sprigs, to balance the dark and light aspects.

Creative Art Projects

- Encourage children to draw or paint Krampus in a way that feels playful rather than frightening.
- Display these artworks around the home as part of your holiday decor.

5. Celebrating Krampusnacht
What is Krampusnacht?

- Celebrated on December 5th, Krampusnacht is a traditional event where people honor Krampus through parades, costumes, and rituals.

Hosting a Family-Friendly Krampusnacht

- **Costumes:** Dress as playful versions of Krampus and St. Nicholas.
- **Parades or Plays:** Reenact Krampus folklore with family or friends in a lighthearted and humorous way.
- **Feast and Treats:** Prepare themed foods, such as gingerbread cookies shaped like Krampus or St. Nicholas.

6. Teaching Life Lessons Through Krampus Lore
Kindness and Accountability

- Use Krampus as a symbol to teach children about the value of kindness and the consequences of unkind actions.
- Create a "Kindness Chart" where children earn stars or stickers for good deeds during the Yule season.

Letting Go of Negativity

- Frame Krampus as a figure who helps take away bad habits or negative energy, encouraging personal growth.
- Incorporate rituals where family members write down things they want to release and symbolically "give them to Krampus."

7. Krampus-Themed Activities
Krampus Hunt

- Organize a scavenger hunt where children search for Krampus-themed items or clues hidden around the house or yard.
- Turn the hunt into a teaching moment by tying each item to a positive action or lesson.

Krampus Gift Exchange

- Create a tradition where family members exchange small, humorous "naughty" gifts, such as coal-shaped candies or gag items, alongside their regular gifts.

Story Sharing

- Host a storytelling night where each person shares their own interpretation of a Krampus tale, emphasizing creative and uplifting themes.

8. Rituals to Honor Krampus Safely
Krampus Offering Ritual

1. **Prepare an Offering:** Use seasonal items like bread, nuts, or mulled wine.
2. **Create a Space:** Place the offering outside or in a symbolic location, such as a small altar decorated with Krampus imagery.
3. **Say an Intention:**
   "Krampus of lore, we honor your tale, but within this home, may light prevail. Take this gift as a symbol of peace; in this space, may all harm cease."

Banishing Ritual Post-Krampus Activities

- After hosting Krampus-themed events, perform a banishing ritual to cleanse and reset the energy of your home.
- Use bells, candles, or incense to clear lingering negativity and reaffirm your protective boundaries.

9. Balancing Krampus and St. Nicholas
Dual Celebrations

- Pair Krampus traditions with St. Nicholas festivities to emphasize the balance between light and dark, reward and consequence.

Kindness Letters

- Have children write letters to St. Nicholas about their good deeds while reflecting on what behaviors they would like to improve.

Collaborative Decorations

- Create decorations that feature both Krampus and St. Nicholas, symbolizing harmony and duality in the holiday season.

10. Ensuring a Positive Experience
Focus on Fun and Growth

- Keep activities lighthearted and enjoyable, avoiding anything that might scare or unsettle participants.

Monitor Energy

- If you notice tension or discomfort during Krampus-themed activities, pause and reset with a focus on positivity.

Celebrate Achievements

- Use Krampus lore as an opportunity to recognize and celebrate acts of kindness and personal growth during the season.

Conclusion: Honoring Without Inviting

Incorporating Krampus lore into your Yule traditions can add depth and creativity to your celebrations, but it's essential to approach the myth with care and intention. By focusing on storytelling, crafts, and life lessons, you can honor the legend of Krampus in a way that is safe, meaningful, and family-friendly. As you weave his story into your festivities, remember that the true spirit of Yule lies in the balance between light and dark, joy and reflection, and the warmth of family and tradition.

Part VI: Aftermath and Reassurance

Chapter 23: Surviving a Krampus Encounter
What to Do If Krampus Gets Through Your Defenses.
Introduction: Preparing for the Unthinkable

Even with the most robust Krampusproofing strategies, there's always a chance that the mischievous and malevolent Krampus could find a way into your space. While folklore paints him as a fearsome figure, there are steps you can take to survive a Krampus encounter safely. Whether by outsmarting him, appeasing his darker tendencies, or banishing him outright, this chapter provides detailed strategies for dealing with Krampus if he breaches your defenses.

1. Understanding Krampus's Motives and Weaknesses
What Drives Krampus?

- **Punishment for Misdeeds:** Krampus targets those deemed "naughty" or morally lacking, according to folklore.
- **Chaos and Mischief:** He thrives on fear, disorder, and negativity.
- **Symbolism of Balance:** Krampus represents the darker side of the season, meant to remind us of the consequences of bad behavior.

Weaknesses

- **Symbols of Light and Purity:** Candles, bells, and holy symbols can repel him.
- **Kindness and Positivity:** Acts of genuine goodwill and generosity weaken his influence.
- **Protective Wards:** Certain herbs, charms, and sigils are believed to neutralize his power.

2. First Steps: Stay Calm and Assess the Situation
Do Not Panic

- Fear feeds Krampus's energy. Remaining calm and composed will help weaken his hold on the situation.

Evaluate the Signs

- Look for indicators that Krampus has entered your space:
    - Unusual noises, such as chains rattling or deep growls.
    - Sudden temperature drops or eerie shadows.
    - Disturbed areas of the home, such as broken ornaments or scattered objects.

Gather Your Tools

- **Keep a prepared kit of protective items nearby, including:**
    - Bells and candles.
    - Sage, salt, or protective herbs.
    - A written or memorized banishing chant.

3. Strategies for Confronting Krampus
Appeasement Rituals

- **Offer a Gift: Folklore suggests that Krampus can be appeased with offerings of food or drink.**
    - Place bread, fruit, or mulled wine on a small plate and leave it near your hearth or door.
    - Recite:
    "Krampus of shadow, hear my plea; take this gift and let us be. With this offering, I make amends; no harm shall come, let this night end."

Show Kindness

- **Repent and Reflect: Acknowledge personal faults or misdeeds and express a desire to improve.**
    - Say aloud:
    "Krampus, I see my wrongs and strive to be better. Take with you my regrets and leave behind peace."

Redirect His Energy

- **Set a Decoy: Create a symbolic "naughty figure" using a scarecrow or a stuffed figure. Place it outside your home with a note explaining it as a gift to Krampus.**
    - Include items that represent negativity you wish to banish, such as slips of paper with bad habits or worries written on them.

4. Banishing Krampus

If appeasement fails, banishing Krampus becomes essential. This requires invoking protective energy and expelling him from your space.

The Banishing Ritual

1. **Gather Materials:** A black candle, bells, sage or rosemary, and salt.
2. **Light the Candle:** Place it in the room where Krampus's presence feels strongest.
3. **Burn Sage or Rosemary:** Walk around the space, allowing the smoke to fill the area.
4. **Ring Bells:** Use a bell to create vibrations that break up his energy.
5. **Recite the Banishing Chant:**
   "By the light of fire, the sound of chime, leave this space, foul one, it's time. No shadow shall linger, no harm shall stay; by the power of Yule, be gone this day!"
6. **Sprinkle Salt:** Create a line of salt at doorways and windows to seal the space against re-entry.

5. Escaping and Seeking Help

If You Feel Overwhelmed

- Retreat to a secure room or location. Bring protective items, such as candles and bells, with you.
- Call upon family members or spiritual practitioners for assistance.

Contacting Spiritual Allies

- Invoke protective deities or spirits through prayer or offerings. For example:
    - Thor for strength and courage.
    - Brigid for hearth and home protection.
    - Archangel Michael for divine intervention.

6. Post-Encounter Cleansing and Restoration
Cleansing Your Home

- After banishing Krampus, perform a thorough cleansing to remove lingering negativity.
    - Smudge the home with sage or cedar.
    - Light white candles in each room.
    - Sprinkle salt or protective herbs in corners and along thresholds.

Reinforcing Defenses

- Refresh protective charms, wreaths, and symbols around your home.
- Perform a house blessing to restore harmony and peace:
    - Recite:
      "This home is sacred, this space is blessed. No shadow or harm shall ever nest."

Reflect and Adjust

- Consider whether any weaknesses in your Krampusproofing measures need improvement.
- Use the experience as an opportunity to strengthen your spiritual practices.

7. Turning Fear into Strength
Learn from the Encounter

- Reflect on what Krampus represents in your life. Are there habits, fears, or negativity that need addressing?
- Use his symbolism as a catalyst for personal growth and renewal.

Celebrate Survival

- Host a post-encounter gathering with family or friends to celebrate resilience and positivity.
- Share stories, light candles, and reaffirm your protective practices.

Conclusion: Emerging Stronger from the Shadows

A Krampus encounter may seem daunting, but with preparation, composure, and the right tools, you can navigate the experience safely and even grow from it. By understanding his symbolic role and taking proactive measures, you turn what could be a fearful event into an opportunity for renewal and empowerment. Surviving Krampus isn't just about repelling darkness—it's about embracing the light within yourself and your home, ensuring that your Yule season remains a time of joy, harmony, and triumph over adversity.

Part VI: Aftermath and Reassurance

Chapter 24: Healing and Restoring Your Space
Rituals and Practices to Cleanse Your Home After a Krampus Incident
Introduction: Why Healing and Cleansing Matter

After a Krampus incident or any unsettling experience, your home may retain residual negativity or feel energetically imbalanced. Healing and restoring your space is essential to dispel lingering dark energy, repair spiritual boundaries, and invite positive energy back into your home. These rituals not only cleanse but also re-establish your home as a sanctuary of peace and safety.

This chapter provides detailed steps for spiritual and practical restoration, including cleansing rituals, energy alignment practices, and protective measures to rebuild harmony and strength in your living space.

1. Signs Your Space Needs Healing
Energetic Imbalances

- A heavy or oppressive feeling in certain areas of the home.
- Difficulty concentrating or feeling anxious without clear cause.
- Stagnant or cold areas, despite heating or airflow.

Physical Indicators

- Items misplaced or broken during the encounter.
- Unexplained messes, disturbances, or damaged protective barriers.

Emotional Residue

- Lingering fear or discomfort, especially for children or pets.
- Increased tension or arguments among family members.

2. Preparing for the Cleansing Process
Physical Cleanup

- Clear debris, broken items, or anything disturbed during the Krampus encounter.
- Wash or replace soft furnishings like curtains, blankets, or cushions if they feel energetically "heavy."

Gathering Tools

- **Candles:** White for purification, black to dispel negativity, and green for renewal.
- **Incense or Herbs:** Sage, cedar, rosemary, or frankincense for cleansing and protection.
- **Crystals:** Black tourmaline for absorbing negativity, clear quartz for amplification, and rose quartz for emotional healing.
- **Salt:** For creating barriers and absorbing residual energy.

• **Bells or Chimes:** To break up stagnant energy.

Setting Intentions

• Clearly state your goals for the cleansing ritual, such as:
    ◦ *"I release all negativity from this space and invite peace and harmony."*
    ◦ *"This home is restored and protected, free from all harm."*

3. Step-by-Step Cleansing Rituals
The Complete Home Cleansing Ritual

1. **Begin at the Threshold:**
    ◦ Stand at your front door with a lit white candle and say:
    "This home is a sanctuary, and no darkness may remain."
    ◦ Ring a bell or clap your hands to signify the start of the cleansing.
2. **Cleanse Each Room:**
    ◦ Walk clockwise through each room with burning sage or incense, focusing on corners, windows, and doorways.
    ◦ Say:
    "I cleanse this space of all negativity. Only light and love may dwell here."
    ◦ Use a bell or chime to disperse stagnant energy in dense areas.
3. **Sprinkle Salt:**
    ◦ Sprinkle salt along windowsills, thresholds, and in the corners of each room to absorb and block negative energy.
4. **Light Renewal Candles:**
    ◦ Place green candles in central areas of your home and light them as a symbol of renewal and growth.
5. **End with Gratitude:**
    ◦ Thank any protective spirits or deities you invoked for their assistance.

The Elemental Cleansing Ritual

• **Purpose:** Utilize the power of earth, air, fire, and water to restore balance.

1. **Earth:**
    ◦ Sprinkle salt or place grounding crystals (like black tourmaline) in key areas of the home.
2. **Air:**
    ◦ Burn cleansing herbs or incense to purify the air.
3. **Fire:**
    ◦ Light a black candle to absorb negativity and a white candle to symbolize renewal.

4. **Water:**
- Fill a bowl with water and a few drops of essential oil (like lavender or rosemary).
- Use a branch of cedar or pine to sprinkle the water around the home while reciting a blessing:
  "By water's flow, I cleanse this space; by fire's light, I renew its grace."

Emergency Energy Reset

- If you feel a lingering dark presence, perform this quick ritual:
  1. Ring a loud bell or bang on a pot in every corner of the home.
  2. Follow with sage or cedar smoke to clear the disrupted energy.
  3. Sprinkle salt on the floor and sweep it up, visualizing negativity being swept away.

4. Emotional Healing for the Household
For Children

- Reassure children that the home is now protected and safe.
- Encourage them to participate in a simple activity, such as decorating a protective charm or drawing symbols of peace.

For Pets

- Pets often sense lingering energy. Spend time comforting them and creating a calm environment.
- Place amethyst or rose quartz near their sleeping area for soothing energy.

For Adults

- Reflect on the experience and release any residual fear through journaling or meditation.
- Perform a personal cleansing ritual, such as a salt bath or smudging your aura with sage.

5. Rebuilding Protective Barriers
Physical Barriers

- Replace any damaged protective charms, wreaths, or sigils around your home.
- Hang bells or wind chimes near entry points to maintain a constant flow of protective energy.

Symbolic Barriers

- Draw protective sigils or runes (such as Algiz) on doors and windows using chalk or invisible ink.

• Create a salt line around the perimeter of your home and reinforce it with protective herbs.

Crystals and Talismans

• Place black tourmaline near entry points to absorb and repel negative energy.
• Add clear quartz and citrine to your Yule altar or mantle to amplify positive energy.

6. Rituals for Inviting Positive Energy
The Yule Gratitude Ceremony

1. Gather family members around a lit candle and take turns sharing something you're grateful for.
2. Offer a toast or small gift to the home itself, symbolizing your intention to nurture and protect it.

The Harmony Ring Ritual

1. Stand in a circle with your family and hold hands.
2. Recite together:
   "From shadow to light, from fear to peace, we bless this home with love's release."

7. Seasonal Maintenance for Lasting Peace
Weekly Cleansing

• Smudge your home with sage or cedar once a week during the Yule season.

Recharging Protective Items

• Place crystals and talismans under moonlight or sunlight to refresh their energy.

Daily Affirmations

• Light a candle each morning and say:
  "This home is a haven of love, peace, and joy."

8. Recognizing the Return of Balance
Signs of Harmony

• A lighter, calmer atmosphere in your home.
• Family members feeling more connected and at ease.
• Pets returning to normal behavior, such as sleeping soundly or playing.

Increased Positivity

- Opportunities, joyful moments, and an overall sense of well-being become more frequent.

Conclusion: Restoring Your Sanctuary

Healing and restoring your space after a Krampus incident is more than just cleansing—it's about reclaiming your home as a place of safety, warmth, and joy. By performing these rituals and practices, you not only banish lingering negativity but also strengthen your home's defenses and invite lasting harmony. With your space renewed and fortified, you can fully embrace the spirit of Yule, celebrating light, love, and the triumph of peace over darkness.

Chapter 25: Preparing for Next Yule
Building a Tradition of Protection and Joy for Future Celebrations
Introduction: Laying the Foundation for Future Yule Seasons

As the current Yule season comes to a close, preparing for next year ensures that your home remains a sanctuary of protection, peace, and joy. By reflecting on the past year, refining your rituals, and creating a legacy of meaningful traditions, you set the stage for celebrations that strengthen your family bonds and safeguard against negativity. Preparation is not just practical—it's a spiritual investment in the continued prosperity and harmony of your household.

This chapter explores how to carry forward the lessons and practices of this Yule season, establish enduring traditions, and strengthen your Krampusproofing measures for years to come.

1. Reflecting on This Yule Season
Evaluating Your Successes

- Reflect on what worked well this Yule season:
    - Which rituals brought the most peace and protection?
    - What traditions did your family enjoy the most?

Identifying Areas for Improvement

- Consider what could be enhanced:
    - Were there gaps in your protective measures?
    - Did you feel any lingering negativity or challenges?

Recording Your Experience

- Keep a Yule journal to document:
    - Rituals performed and their outcomes.
    - Memorable moments and lessons learned.
    - Ideas for improving future celebrations.

2. Strengthening Your Protective Practices
Reviewing Your Krampusproofing Measures

- Evaluate the effectiveness of your defenses:
    ◦ Did your protective charms, sigils, or rituals hold strong?
    ◦ Were there areas of your home that felt more vulnerable?

Updating Protective Tools

- Refresh or replace worn charms, wreaths, and symbols.
- Create new sigils or talismans based on lessons from this year.

Enhancing Your Perimeter

- Reinforce physical and symbolic barriers:
    ◦ Add evergreen plants or protective herbs like rosemary and holly around your property.
    ◦ Use salt or chalk to renew protective lines at windows and doorways.

3. Creating Enduring Traditions
Designing Family Rituals

- Develop rituals that your family looks forward to each year:
    ◦ A Yule blessing ceremony at the hearth.
    ◦ A family craft day to create protective ornaments or charms.
    ◦ A storytelling night featuring Krampus lore or Yule myths.

Involving Everyone

- Assign roles to family members to make traditions interactive:
    ◦ Children can ring bells or light candles during protective rituals.
    ◦ Adults can lead blessings or craft protective items.

Celebrating Gratitude

- Establish a tradition of sharing gratitude as part of your Yule preparations.
    ◦ Example: Create a "Yule Gratitude Jar" where everyone writes something they're thankful for throughout the season.

4. Preparing Your Home for Next Year
Organizing Yule Supplies

- Store candles, herbs, charms, and other ritual items in a dedicated Yule box.
- Label and organize decorations, ensuring they're ready for next year.

Creating a Yule Prep Checklist

- Include tasks like:
    - Refreshing charms and sigils.
    - Gathering herbs and incense for cleansing.
    - Planning seasonal meals and activities.

Decorating with Intention

- Plan decorations that incorporate protection and positivity:
    - Use red and white ribbons for strength and purity.
    - Add symbols of light, such as sun-shaped ornaments or star motifs.

5. Building Your Yule Wardrobe
Crafting Protective Clothing

- Create garments or accessories that double as protection:
    - Embroider clothing with protective runes or sigils.
    - Incorporate bells, evergreen sprigs, or red ribbons into scarves and hats.

Yule-Themed Accessories

- Develop a collection of festive jewelry or pins featuring protective symbols, such as penta-grams, holly, or runes.

6. Strengthening Spiritual Practices Year-Round
Daily Energy Cleansing

- Incorporate simple practices into your daily routine, such as:
    - Lighting a candle and reciting a short affirmation each morning.
    - Smudging your space with sage or cedar weekly.

Seasonal Maintenance

- Perform a thorough cleansing and blessing of your home at key times, such as the spring equinox, midsummer, and autumn equinox.

Developing a Spiritual Connection

- Strengthen your relationship with protective spirits or deities through regular offerings, meditations, or prayers.

7. Preparing for Next Krampusnacht
Planning Family-Friendly Activities

- Organize Krampus-themed events that are fun and safe:
    - A scavenger hunt featuring Krampus lore.
    - Baking Krampus-inspired cookies or treats.

Refreshing Your Knowledge

- Research new stories, myths, or cultural traditions related to Krampus and Yule to incorporate into your celebrations.

Revisiting Protective Measures

- Ensure your defenses are ready to repel Krampus if needed:
    - Strengthen symbolic barriers like salt lines, wreaths, and charms.
    - Refresh your banishing chants and rituals.

8. Fostering Community Connections
Sharing Yule Traditions

- Host gatherings or potlucks with neighbors or friends to share protective rituals and celebrate the season.

Teaching Protective Practices

- Offer workshops or informal lessons on creating charms, sigils, or Yule decorations.

Supporting Local Traditions

- Participate in local Krampusnacht parades or Yule markets to connect with your community and honor the season's folklore.

9. Creating a Legacy of Joy and Protection
Passing Traditions to the Next Generation

- Involve children in crafting and rituals to ensure they carry forward family traditions.
- Share stories about the meaning behind your Yule practices, emphasizing protection, love, and harmony.

Building a Yule Book of Shadows

- Document your family's Yule rituals, protective spells, and favorite traditions in a special book.
- Include notes on what worked well each year and ideas for improvement.

Committing to Annual Renewal

- Use each Yule season as an opportunity to renew your family's commitment to positivity and protection.

10. Setting Intentions for the Year Ahead
Manifesting Peace and Abundance

- Perform a New Year's Yule ritual to set intentions for the coming year:
    ◦ Light a green candle for growth and prosperity.
    ◦ Write down goals and affirmations, then place them on your Yule altar.

Cultivating Gratitude

- Start a gratitude practice, such as journaling or sharing moments of appreciation with family.

Reinforcing Your Home's Energy

- Conclude the Yule season with a final blessing to seal the energy of your home:
    ◦ Say:
    "As this Yule season ends, we carry its light into the days ahead. This home remains a haven of peace, protection, and joy."

Conclusion: The Spirit of Preparedness
Preparing for next Yule is not just about safeguarding your home but about building a lasting tradition of joy, protection, and connection. By reflecting on your experiences, refining your practices, and involving your family and community, you create a Yule celebration that grows richer and more meaningful each year. Embrace the opportunity to turn lessons into legacy, ensuring that the warmth and light of Yule guide you through every season to come.

Appendices

Appendix A: Yule Protection Recipes and Spells

Step-by-Step Instructions for Protective Potions, Charms, and Incenses

Introduction: Crafting Your Protective Tools

Yule is a season rich in magical energy, making it the perfect time to create protective potions, charms, and incenses. These handcrafted tools enhance your rituals, shield your home from negativity, and ensure a harmonious and safe environment. This appendix provides detailed, step-by-step recipes and spells to help you prepare protective items infused with the spirit of Yule.

1. Protective Potions for Yule

A. Hearth Protection Potion

Purpose: To protect the hearth, the symbolic heart of the home, from negative energies.

Ingredients:

- 1 cup water (preferably spring water)
- 1 tablespoon dried rosemary
- 1 tablespoon dried cinnamon bark
- 1 teaspoon salt
- 3 drops of frankincense essential oil

Steps:

1. In a small pot, bring the water to a gentle boil.
2. Add the rosemary, cinnamon bark, and salt. Stir clockwise.
3. Reduce heat and let simmer for 10 minutes.
4. Remove from heat, allow to cool slightly, and strain the liquid into a glass jar.
5. Add three drops of frankincense essential oil and shake gently.
6. Use the potion to anoint your hearthstone or fireplace with a sprig of evergreen, saying:
   "Hearth of this home, burn bright and pure, may no harm enter, may light endure."

B. Doorway Guardian Potion
Purpose: To create a protective barrier at entry points.
Ingredients:

- **1 cup apple cider vinegar**
- **1 tablespoon dried thyme**
- **1 tablespoon dried lavender**
- **5 drops of cedarwood essential oil**

Steps:

1. **Combine all ingredients in a clean glass bottle.**
2. **Shake vigorously to mix.**
3. **Sprinkle a small amount of the potion along windowsills and doorways, reciting:**
   "Through this threshold, none may pass who bring harm or ill to my kin and glass."
4. **Store the remaining potion in a dark, cool place for future use.**

2. Protective Charms and Talismans
A. Krampus Banishing Charm
Purpose: To repel Krampus or other malevolent forces during Yule.
Materials:

- A small fabric pouch (red or black)
- 1 tablespoon dried holly leaves
- 1 teaspoon salt
- 1 small bell
- A small piece of iron or nail

Steps:

1. Place the holly leaves, salt, bell, and iron inside the pouch.
2. Tie the pouch shut with red ribbon, focusing on your intention to repel negativity.
3. Hold the charm in your hands and say:
   "With holly and salt, with bell and iron, no harm may linger, no darkness environ."
4. Hang the charm near the hearth, doorways, or any vulnerable area.

B. Family Harmony Charm
Purpose: To foster peace and harmony among family members during Yule.
Materials:

- A small crystal (amethyst or rose quartz)
- 3 bay leaves
- A sprig of cedar
- White fabric pouch

Steps:

1. Place the crystal, bay leaves, and cedar sprig in the pouch.
2. Tie it closed with white ribbon.
3. Hold the charm and say:
   "Harmony and peace, fill this home, where love resides, no ill shall roam."
4. Hang or place the charm in a central room to promote unity and tranquility.

3. Protective Incenses for Yule
A. Cleansing and Protection Incense
Purpose: To cleanse and shield your home during Yule rituals.
Ingredients:

- **2 tablespoons dried rosemary**
- **1 tablespoon dried sage**
- **1 tablespoon pine needles (dried)**
- **1 teaspoon frankincense resin**

Steps:

1. **Crush all ingredients into a fine powder using a mortar and pestle.**
2. **Store in an airtight jar until ready to use.**
3. **Sprinkle a small amount onto burning charcoal in a heat-safe incense burner.**
4. **Waft the smoke through each room, reciting:**
   "Smoke of sage and pine, cleanse this space, protect what's mine."

B. Hearth Blessing Incense
Purpose: To bless and protect the hearth as the heart of the home.
Ingredients:

- **1 tablespoon dried cinnamon**
- **1 tablespoon dried orange peel**
- **1 teaspoon clove powder**
- **1 teaspoon myrrh resin**

Steps:

1. **Combine all ingredients in a mortar and pestle and grind into a fine powder.**
2. **Store in a glass jar.**
3. **Sprinkle a small amount on burning charcoal in the hearth, saying:**
   "Bless this hearth, warm and bright, a beacon of love through Yule's long night."

4. Yule Protection Spells
A. The Salt Circle Spell
Purpose: To create a temporary protective barrier for your home or ritual space.
Materials:

- Salt
- 1 white candle

Steps:

1. Light the white candle and place it in the center of the area you wish to protect.
2. Slowly sprinkle salt in a circle around the perimeter, visualizing a glowing shield of light.
3. As you complete the circle, say:
   "With salt and flame, this space I seal, no harm may enter, no ill shall steal."

B. The Evergreen Protection Spell
Purpose: To guard your home and family throughout the Yule season.
Materials:

- A bundle of evergreen branches (holly, cedar, pine)
- Red ribbon
- A small bell

Steps:

1. Tie the evergreen branches together with the red ribbon, attaching the bell to the bundle.
2. Hang the bundle above your front door or on your hearth mantle.
3. Stand before the bundle and say:
   "Evergreen strong, winter's shield, guard this home, your power yield. By ribbon red and bell's chime clear, no harm may dwell, no dark draw near."

5. Tips for Maximizing Effectiveness

- Set Intentions Clearly: Before starting any recipe or spell, focus your mind on your desired outcome.
- Cleanse Tools and Materials: Smudge herbs, crystals, and other items to remove residual energies before use.

• **Repeat Rituals:** Perform these spells and recipes periodically throughout the Yule season to maintain their potency.

Conclusion: Crafting a Shield of Light

The recipes and spells in this appendix are designed to empower you to create a safe, harmonious, and joyful environment during Yule. By combining the symbolic power of herbs, crystals, and intention with ancient traditions, you strengthen your home's defenses and infuse your space with light and love. Let these tools serve as a foundation for your Yule preparations, ensuring peace and protection for years to come.

Appendix B: Traditional Krampus Lore and Artifacts
A Deeper Dive into Historical Artifacts and Their Modern Interpretations
Introduction: The Enduring Mystery of Krampus

Krampus, the horned and fearsome figure of Alpine folklore, is a complex symbol of winter traditions that balance light and dark. His story has been passed down through generations, often accompanied by unique artifacts that reflect the region's rich cultural heritage. Understanding these artifacts and their historical significance provides deeper insight into Krampus lore while exploring how they are interpreted in modern times.

This appendix examines the historical artifacts associated with Krampus, their symbolism, and how they are celebrated today, offering a comprehensive understanding of his place in Yule traditions.

1. The Origins of Krampus Lore
Roots in Pagan Rituals

- Krampus likely originated from pre-Christian Alpine traditions that celebrated the winter solstice.
- He is thought to be connected to fertility and wilderness spirits, embodying nature's untamed and chaotic aspects.

Integration with Christian Festivities

- With the rise of Christianity, Krampus was integrated into St. Nicholas traditions, taking on the role of punishing the wicked while St. Nicholas rewarded the virtuous.
- This duality symbolized the balance between reward and consequence during the holiday season.

2. Historical Artifacts Associated with Krampus
A. The Krampus Mask

- **Description:** Hand-carved wooden masks depicting Krampus's demonic face, often with exaggerated features such as horns, fangs, and long tongues.
- **Historical Context:** Masks were used in Krampusnacht celebrations, where participants dressed as Krampus to parade through villages.
- **Symbolism:** The mask's grotesque features are meant to instill fear, reinforcing the moral lessons of Krampus lore.
- **Modern Interpretation:** Today, masks are both ceremonial and collectible, with artisans crafting elaborate designs for Krampus parades and festivals.

B. Birch Rods (Ruten)

- **Description:** Bundles of birch twigs carried by Krampus, traditionally used to swat misbehaving children.
- **Historical Context:** The birch rod symbolizes both discipline and fertility, reflecting Krampus's dual nature as punisher and nature spirit.
- **Symbolism:** The twigs are a reminder of the consequences of bad behavior, while their connection to trees ties Krampus to the natural world.
- **Modern Interpretation:** Birch rods are often decorative, tied with red ribbons and used as part of Krampus-themed decorations.

C. Chains

- **Description:** Heavy metal chains carried or worn by Krampus, sometimes adorned with bells.
- **Historical Context:** Chains were introduced to Krampus imagery as a Christian symbol of binding the devil, signifying the triumph of good over evil.
- **Symbolism:** The clanking chains serve as both a warning of Krampus's approach and a reminder of the consequences of unbridled behavior.
- **Modern Interpretation:** Chains remain a prominent feature in Krampus costumes, symbolizing his menacing presence while adding dramatic flair to parades.

D. Bells (Krampus Glocken)

- **Description:** Large, loud cowbells worn by Krampus around the waist or carried in hand.
- **Historical Context:** Bells were used to announce Krampus's arrival and to ward off evil spirits during winter festivals.
- **Symbolism:** The sound of the bells disrupts negative energies and acts as both a tool of fear and protection.
- **Modern Interpretation:** Bells are still an integral part of Krampus parades, adding auditory drama to the visual spectacle.

E. Krampus Cards (Krampuskarten)

- **Description:** Illustrated postcards featuring Krampus, popular in the late 19th and early 20th centuries.
- **Historical Context:** These cards were part of the Austrian and German tradition of sending holiday greetings, often depicting Krampus chasing, punishing, or carrying away misbehaving children.
- **Symbolism:** The cards combined humor, moral lessons, and the festive spirit, blending Krampus's darker aspects with holiday cheer.
- **Modern Interpretation:** Krampus cards are highly collectible today, with vintage designs sought after by enthusiasts and new designs continuing the tradition.

3. Modern Krampus Artifacts and Celebrations
A. Krampus Costumes

- **Description:** Full-body costumes featuring fur, horns, masks, and accessories like chains and bells.
- **Purpose:** Worn during Krampusnacht parades to reenact traditional folklore.
- **Cultural Significance:** The costumes preserve cultural heritage while offering participants an immersive experience in Krampus lore.

B. Decorative Ornaments

- **Description:** Krampus-themed ornaments, including figurines, tree decorations, and wreath embellishments.
- **Purpose:** Incorporate Krampus imagery into modern Yule or Christmas celebrations.
- **Cultural Significance:** These items allow individuals to honor the folklore in a lighthearted and festive way.

C. Krampus Festivals and Markets

- **Description:** Events featuring Krampus parades, markets selling Krampus-themed goods, and storytelling.
- **Purpose:** To celebrate and preserve the folklore while engaging modern audiences.
- **Cultural Significance:** Festivals like those in Austria, Germany, and the United States (e.g., in cities like Los Angeles) showcase the global appeal of Krampus traditions.

4. Symbolism of Krampus Artifacts
Duality

- Krampus artifacts emphasize the balance between light and dark, reward and punishment, and order and chaos.

Cultural Identity

- The craftsmanship of Krampus masks, costumes, and cards reflects the rich cultural heritage of Alpine regions.

Modern Revival

- Krampus artifacts have gained renewed popularity as symbols of alternative holiday celebrations, appealing to those who appreciate darker or more unconventional traditions.

5. Collecting and Preserving Krampus Artifacts
Tips for Collectors

- Seek out authentic handmade masks and costumes from artisans in Alpine regions.
- Look for vintage Krampus cards from Austria and Germany, often found at antique markets or online auctions.

Caring for Artifacts

- Store masks and costumes in a cool, dry place to preserve their materials.
- Display postcards and other paper artifacts in acid-free frames to protect them from light and humidity.

Ethical Considerations

- Support artisans who use sustainable and traditional methods in crafting Krampus items.

6. Incorporating Artifacts into Modern Celebrations
Home Decor

- Use Krampus ornaments, wreaths, and birch bundles as part of your Yule decorations.
- Create a display featuring Krampus cards or small figurines to honor the folklore.

Themed Events

- Host a Krampusnacht party with costumes, storytelling, and festive foods.
- Use chains, bells, and masks as props to set the scene.

Educational Opportunities

- Share the history and significance of Krampus artifacts with family and friends to keep the tradition alive.
- Incorporate Krampus lore into holiday lessons or activities for children, focusing on the cultural and moral aspects.

Conclusion: Preserving and Honoring Krampus Lore

Krampus artifacts are more than just symbols of folklore—they are a tangible connection to centuries-old traditions and cultural identity. By understanding their historical significance and modern interpretations, you can honor the rich tapestry of Krampus lore while integrating it into your Yule celebrations. Whether through collecting, crafting, or storytelling, these artifacts ensure that Krampus's story continues to inspire and captivate future generations.

Appendix C: Protective Symbols and Their Meanings
Detailed Explanations of Sigils, Runes, and Other Symbols Discussed in the Book
Introduction: The Power of Symbols in Protection

Symbols have been used for centuries as tools of protection, empowerment, and spiritual alignment. Whether drawn, carved, or worn as amulets, these sacred signs hold significant energy and intent. This appendix provides detailed explanations of the protective symbols, sigils, and runes mentioned in this book, offering a deeper understanding of their meanings and how to use them effectively in your rituals and practices.

1. Sigils: Personal Symbols of Intention
What Are Sigils?

- Sigils are unique, personalized symbols created to embody a specific intention or desire.
- They are often used in modern magick practices to focus energy and manifest goals.

Creating a Protective Sigil

1. Write your intention, such as "My home is protected from harm."
2. Remove duplicate letters, leaving a simplified version of the phrase.
3. Combine the remaining letters into a unique design.
4. Charge the sigil by focusing your energy on it during meditation or ritual.

Example Protective Sigil

- A circle enclosing an abstract pattern that represents unity, boundaries, and defense against negativity.

2. Runes: Ancient Symbols of Protection

Runes are ancient letters of the Germanic alphabet, often used for divination and protection. Below are some key protective runes and their meanings.

A. Algiz (◈)

- **Meaning:** Protection, defense, and shielding.
- **Use:** Carve or draw this rune on doors, windows, or personal items to ward off harm.
- **Symbolism:** Often associated with an elk's antlers, representing vigilance and guardianship.

B. Thurisaz (◈)

- **Meaning:** Power, defense, and destruction of threats.
- **Use:** Invoke Thurisaz during rituals to repel malevolent forces or clear obstacles.
- **Symbolism:** Linked to Thor's hammer, it embodies strength and action.

C. Eihwaz (◈)

- **Meaning:** Endurance, resilience, and transformation.
- **Use:** Draw Eihwaz on charms or protective amulets to foster spiritual strength and perseverance.
- **Symbolism:** Often associated with the yew tree, symbolizing longevity and protection.

D. Sowilo (◈)

- **Meaning:** Light, victory, and positive energy.
- **Use:** Place Sowilo near the hearth or in central areas to dispel darkness and invite light.
- **Symbolism:** The sun's rays, representing triumph over adversity.

3. Pentagrams and Pentacles

Pentagram

- **Meaning:** Balance, protection, and connection to the five elements (earth, air, fire, water, spirit).
- **Use:** Draw or wear a pentagram during rituals to create a protective barrier.

Pentacle

- **Meaning:** A pentagram enclosed in a circle, symbolizing unity and infinite protection.
- **Use:** Place a pentacle on your altar or doors to guard against negativity and invite harmony.

4. Cultural Symbols of Protection
A. The Eye of Horus (Egyptian)

- **Meaning:** Protection, healing, and divine insight.
- **Use:** Place the Eye of Horus near entryways or wear it as jewelry to guard against harm and enhance spiritual awareness.

B. Hamsa Hand (Middle Eastern)

- **Meaning:** Protection from the "evil eye" and blessings of luck and prosperity.
- **Use:** Hang a Hamsa symbol in your home or wear it to repel malevolent intentions and attract positivity.

C. Triskelion (Celtic)

- **Meaning:** Protection, balance, and the cycle of life.
- **Use:** Incorporate the Triskelion in charms or decorations to align with the natural flow of energy and guard against disruptions.

5. Sacred Geometry in Protection
Circle

- **Meaning:** Unity, wholeness, and infinite protection.
- **Use:** Draw or create a circle during rituals to establish a sacred boundary.

Triangle

- **Meaning:** Strength, stability, and harmony.
- **Use:** Use upward triangles for growth and empowerment; use downward triangles for grounding and protection.

Hexagram (Star of David)

- **Meaning:** Balance between opposites (spiritual and physical realms).
- **Use:** Incorporate hexagrams in protective talismans or sigils for holistic defense.

6. Protective Christian Symbols
The Cross

- **Meaning:** Divine protection, salvation, and faith.
- **Use:** Place a cross over doorways or wear it as an amulet to invoke divine guardianship.

Circle with a Cross

- **Meaning:** Unity of the physical and spiritual realms.
- **Use:** Include this symbol in protective charms or engravings for balance and harmony.

Archangel Michael's Sword

- **Meaning:** Strength, courage, and defense against evil.
- **Use:** Visualize Archangel Michael's sword cutting through negativity during rituals.

7. Protective Symbols from Nature
Evergreen Branches

- **Meaning:** Resilience, renewal, and protection.
- **Use:** Hang evergreen wreaths or branches near entryways to guard against negativity.

Holly

- **Meaning:** Defense and vitality.
- **Use:** Incorporate holly in wreaths or talismans to ward off malevolent forces.

Pinecones

- **Meaning:** Fertility, wisdom, and protection.
- **Use:** Place pinecones on your altar or in your home to attract positive energy and shield against harm.

8. Practical Applications of Symbols
Drawing and Placement

- Draw symbols on doorframes, windows, or hearthstones using chalk or saltwater.
- Carve them into candles or wooden items to incorporate them into rituals.

Wearing Symbols

- Wear jewelry or clothing adorned with protective symbols to carry their energy with you.

Crafting Talismans

- Combine symbols into a single charm or talisman for amplified protection.

9. Modern Use of Protective Symbols
In Home Decor

- Incorporate symbols into art, ornaments, or everyday items like coasters or tablecloths.

In Digital Spaces

- Use symbols as part of digital wallpapers or designs to create a virtual shield for your devices.

In Meditation

- Focus on a symbol during meditation to align with its protective energy and intention.

Conclusion: Empowering Your Practice with Symbols

Protective symbols are timeless tools for channeling energy, manifesting intentions, and creating sacred boundaries. By understanding their meanings and integrating them into your rituals and daily life, you harness their power to guard your home, family, and spirit. Let these symbols serve as anchors of protection, ensuring that your Yule season—and every season—is filled with light, safety, and harmony.

Appendix D: Resources and Further Reading
Books, Websites, and Communities to Expand Your Knowledge on Krampus and Yule
Introduction: Deepening Your Connection to Krampus and Yule

The lore of Krampus and the traditions of Yule are deeply rooted in history, mythology, and cultural practices. Whether you want to explore the origins of Krampus, expand your knowledge of Yule rituals, or connect with like-minded communities, a wealth of resources is available to guide you. This appendix provides an extensive list of books, websites, and communities to help you delve deeper into the fascinating world of Krampus and Yule.

1. Essential Books on Krampus and Yule
Books on Krampus

1. *The Krampus and the Old, Dark Christmas: Roots and Rebirth of the Folkloric Devil* by Al Ridenour
   - **Overview:** A comprehensive exploration of Krampus's history, cultural significance, and modern revival, written by a leading expert in the field.
   - **Why Read:** This book offers detailed insights into Krampusnacht traditions and the evolution of Krampus as a folkloric figure.
2. *Krampus: The Yule Lord* by Brom
   - **Overview:** A dark fantasy novel blending Krampus lore with modern storytelling.
   - **Why Read:** For those who enjoy fictionalized accounts of folklore, this book offers an imaginative and thrilling take on Krampus.
3. *Beware the Krampus!* by Mike Drake
   - **Overview:** A collection of Krampus-themed short stories written by various authors.
   - **Why Read:** Perfect for those who want a mix of chilling and humorous tales inspired by Krampus.

Books on Yule and Winter Solstice Traditions

1. *The Winter Solstice: The Sacred Traditions of Christmas* by John Matthews
   - **Overview:** A historical look at winter solstice traditions, including Yule and its connection to modern Christmas practices.
   - **Why Read:** This book provides a broader context for understanding Yule's spiritual and cultural significance.
2. *Yule: Rituals, Recipes, & Lore for the Winter Solstice* by Susan Pesznecker
   - **Overview:** Part of the Llewellyn Sabbat Essentials series, this book explores Yule rituals, crafts, and recipes.
   - **Why Read:** A practical guide for those looking to incorporate Yule celebrations into their modern lives.
3. *The Old Magic of Christmas: Yuletide Traditions for the Darkest Days of the Year* by Linda Raedisch
   - **Overview:** A captivating mix of history, folklore, and practical rituals for celebrating Yule.
   - **Why Read:** Combines historical research with modern-day applications, making it ideal for folklore enthusiasts and practitioners.

2. Online Resources
Informational Websites

1. **Krampus.com**
   - **Focus:** A deep dive into Krampus lore, traditions, and cultural practices.
   - **Why Visit:** Features articles, images, and event information for Krampusnacht celebrations worldwide.
2. **History.com's Yule Page**
   - **Focus:** An overview of Yule's history and its transformation into modern holiday traditions.
   - **Why Visit:** Provides accessible, well-researched content for newcomers to Yule traditions.
3. **LearnReligions.com - Yule**
   - **Focus:** Yule rituals, spells, and pagan perspectives.
   - **Why Visit:** Offers practical advice for incorporating Yule into Wiccan or pagan practices.
4. **AlpineFolklore.org**
   - **Focus:** The folklore and traditions of the Alpine region, including Krampus and Perchten figures.
   - **Why Visit:** An excellent resource for understanding the broader cultural context of Krampus.

YouTube Channels and Videos

1. **"The History of Krampus" by TED-Ed**
   - **Overview:** An animated video explaining the origins and cultural significance of Krampus.
   - **Why Watch:** Provides an engaging and educational introduction to Krampus for all ages.
2. **"Yule: Ancient Pagan Origins of Christmas" by Pagan Perspective**
   - **Overview:** A video exploring the pagan roots of Yule and its connection to modern holiday traditions.
   - **Why Watch:** Ideal for those curious about the spiritual side of Yule.
3. **"Krampusnacht Around the World" by Great Big Story**
   - **Overview:** A documentary-style video showcasing modern Krampus celebrations in different countries.
   - **Why Watch:** A visual feast for anyone interested in Krampus's global revival.

3. Communities and Events
Online Communities

1. **Reddit: r/Pagan**
   - **Focus:** Discussions on pagan practices, including Yule rituals and traditions.
   - **Why Join:** A welcoming space to share ideas, ask questions, and learn from experienced practitioners.
2. **Facebook Groups: Yule and Winter Solstice Celebrations**
   - **Focus:** Sharing Yule recipes, rituals, and decorating ideas.
   - **Why Join:** Offers inspiration and support for planning your own Yule celebrations.
3. **Krampusnacht Meetup Groups (via Meetup.com)**
   - **Focus:** Local events and gatherings celebrating Krampusnacht.
   - **Why Join:** Connect with others who share your interest in Krampus and Alpine folklore.

Festivals and Celebrations

1. **Krampusnacht Parades (Austria, Germany, and Beyond)**
   - **Where:** Cities like Salzburg, Vienna, and Munich host elaborate Krampus parades.
   - **Why Attend:** Experience the authentic costumes, rituals, and atmosphere of traditional Krampusnacht.
2. **The Krampus Ball (Los Angeles, USA)**
   - **Focus:** A modern, theatrical take on Krampus celebrations, featuring music, costumes, and performances.

- ◦ **Why Attend:** Perfect for those in North America who want to immerse themselves in Krampus lore.
3. **Pagan Pride Events**
    - ◦ **Focus:** Celebrating pagan traditions, including Yule.
    - ◦ **Why Attend:** A great opportunity to meet like-minded individuals and learn about various winter solstice customs.

4. Academic Resources

1. *The Golden Bough: A Study in Magic and Religion* by Sir James George Frazer
    - ◦ **Overview:** A foundational work exploring seasonal rituals and their mythological significance.
    - ◦ **Why Read:** Offers scholarly insights into the origins of Yule and other solstice celebrations.
2. *Pagan Christmas: The Plants, Spirits, and Rituals at the Origins of Yuletide* by Christian Rätsch and Claudia Müller-Ebeling
    - ◦ **Overview:** A detailed analysis of the pagan roots of Christmas and Yule traditions.
    - ◦ **Why Read:** Perfect for readers seeking an academic yet accessible exploration of the topic.
3. **Journal Articles on Folklore**
    - ◦ Search databases like JSTOR or Project MUSE for articles on Krampus, Yule, and winter solstice traditions.
    - ◦ **Why Read:** Provides well-researched perspectives for those interested in folklore and anthropology.

5. Crafting and DIY Resources
Books

- *The Crafty Witch: Yule Edition* by Willow Hemlock
    - **Focus:** DIY crafts, recipes, and rituals for celebrating Yule creatively.

Websites

- **Pinterest (Yule and Krampus Boards):**
    - **Why Visit:** Find endless inspiration for crafting decorations, charms, and themed gifts.

Workshops and Classes

- Check local metaphysical shops or community centers for Yule crafting or spellcasting workshops.

Conclusion: Expanding Your Knowledge and Practice
Exploring Krampus and Yule is an ongoing journey filled with rich history, captivating folklore, and meaningful rituals. These resources are just the beginning—use them to deepen your understanding, connect with others, and create your own unique traditions. By engaging with these materials, you ensure that the spirit of Krampus and the magic of Yule continue to inspire and enchant for generations to come.

<u>Message from the Author:</u>

I hope you enjoyed this book, I love astrology and knew there was not a book such as this out on the shelf. I love metaphysical items as well. Please check out my other books:

-Life of Government Benefits

-My life of Hell

-My life with Hydrocephalus

-Red Sky

-World Domination:Woman's rule

-World Domination:Woman's Rule 2: The War

-Life and Banishment of Apophis: book 1

-The Kidney Friendly Diet

-The Ultimate Hemp Cookbook

-Creating a Dispensary(legally)

-Cleanliness throughout life: the importance of showering from childhood to adulthood.

-Strong Roots: The Risks of Overcoddling children

-Hemp Horoscopes: Cosmic Insights and Earthly Healing

- Celestial Hemp Navigating the Zodiac: Through the Green Cosmos

-Astrological Hemp: Aligning The Stars with Earth's Ancient Herb

-The Astrological Guide to Hemp: Stars, Signs, and Sacred Leaves

-Green Growth: Innovative Marketing Strategies for your Hemp Products and Dispensary

-Cosmic Cannabis

-Astrological Munchies

-Henry The Hemp

-Zodiacal Roots: The Astrological Soul Of Hemp

- **Green Constellations: Intersection of Hemp and Zodiac**

-Hemp in The Houses: An astrological Adventure Through The Cannabis Galaxy

-Galactic Ganja Guide

Heavenly Hemp

Zodiac Leaves

Doctor Who Astrology

Cannastrology

Stellar Satvias and Cosmic Indicas

Celestial Cannabis: A Zodiac Journey

AstroHerbology: The Sky and The Soil: Volume 1

AstroHerbology:Celestial Cannabis:Volume 2

Cosmic Cannabis Cultivation

The Starry Guide to Herbal Harmony: Volume 1

The Starry Guide to Herbal Harmony: Cannabis Universe: Volume 2

Yugioh Astrology: Astrological Guide to Deck, Duels and more

Nightmare Mansion: Echoes of The Abyss

Nightmare Mansion 2: Legacy of Shadows

Nightmare Mansion 3: Shadows of the Forgotten

Nightmare Mansion 4: Echoes of the Damned

The Life and Banishment of Apophis: Book 2

Nightmare Mansion: Halls of Despair

Healing with Herb: Cannabis and Hydrocephalus

Planetary Pot: Aligning with Astrological Herbs: Volume 1

Fast Track to Freedom: 30 Days to Financial Independence Using AI, Assets, and Agile Hustles

Cosmic Hemp Pathways

How to Become Financially Free in 30 Days: 10,000 Paths to Prosperity

Zodiacal Herbage: Astrological Insights: Volume 1

Nightmare Mansion: Whispers in the Walls

The Daleks Invade Atlantis

Henry the hemp and Hydrocephalus

10X The Kidney Friendly Diet

Cannabis Universe: Adult coloring book

Hemp Astrology: The Healing Power of the Stars

Zodiacal Herbage: Astrological Insights: Cannabis Universe: Volume 2

Planetary Pot: Aligning with Astrological Herbs: Cannabis Universes: Volume 2

Doctor Who Meets the Replicators and SG-1: The Ultimate Battle for Survival

Nightmare Mansion: Curse of the Blood Moon

The Celestial Stoner: A Guide to the Zodiac

Cosmic Pleasures: Sex Toy Astrology for Every Sign

Hydrocephalus Astrology: Navigating the Stars and Healing Waters

Lapis and the Mischievous Chocolate Bar

Celestial Positions: Sexual Astrology for Every Sign

Apophis's Shadow Work Journal: **:** A Journey of Self-Discovery and Healing

Kinky Cosmos: Sexual Kink Astrology for Every Sign

Digital Cosmos: The Astrological Digimon Compendium
Stellar Seeds: The Cosmic Guide to Growing with Astrology
Apophis's Daily Gratitude Journal

Cat Astrology: Feline Mysteries of the Cosmos
The Cosmic Kama Sutra: An Astrological Guide to Sexual Positions
Unleash Your Potential: A Guided Journal Powered by AI Insights
Whispers of the Enchanted Grove

Cosmic Pleasures: An Astrological Guide to Sexual Kinks
369, 12 Manifestation Journal
Whisper of the nocturne journal(blank journal for writing or drawing)
The Boogey Book
Locked In Reflection: A Chastity Journey Through Locktober
Generating Wealth Quickly:
How to Generate $100,000 in 24 Hours
Star Magic: Harness the Power of the Universe
The Flatulence Chronicles: A Fart Journal for Self-Discovery
The Doctor and The Death Moth
Seize the Day: A Personal Seizure Tracking Journal
The Ultimate Boogeyman Safari: A Journey into the Boogie World and Beyond
Whispers of Samhain: 1,000 Spells of Love, Luck, and Lunar Magic: Samhain Spell Book
Apophis's guides:
Witch's Spellbook Crafting Guide for Halloween
<u>Frost & Flame: The Enchanted Yule Grimoire of 1000 Winter Spells</u>
<u>The Ultimate Boogey Goo Guide & Spooky Activities for Halloween Fun</u>
Harmony of the Scales: A Libra's Spellcraft for Balance and Beauty
The Enchanted Advent: 36 Days of Christmas Wonders

Nightmare Mansion: The Labyrinth of Screams
Harvest of Enchantment: 1,000 Spells of Gratitude, Love, and Fortune for Thanksgiving
The Boogey Chronicles: A Journal of Nightly Encounters and Shadowy Secrets
The 12 Days of Financial Freedom: A Step-by-Step Christmas Countdown to Transform Your
Finances
Sigil of the Eternal Spiral Blank Journal
A Christmas Feast: Timeless Recipes for Every Meal
Holiday Stress-Free Solutions: A Survival Guide to Thriving During the Festive Season
Yu-Gi-Oh! Holiday Gifting Mastery: The Ultimate Guide for Fans and Newcomers Alike
Holiday Harmony: A Hydrocephalus Survival Guide for the Festive Season
Celestial Craft: The Witch's Almanac for 2025 – A Cosmic Guide to Manifestations, Moons,
and Mystical Events

Doctor Who: The Toymaker's Winter Wonderland
Tulsa King Unveiled: A Thrilling Guide to Stallone's Mafia Masterpiece
Pendulum Craft: A Complete Guide to Crafting and Using Personalized Divination Tools
Nightmare Mansion: Santa's Eternal Eve
Starlight Noel: A Cosmic Journey through Christmas Mysteries
The Dark Architect: Unlocking the Blueprint of Existence
Surviving the Embrace: The Ultimate Guide to Encounters with The Hugging Molly
The Enchanted Codex: Secrets of the Craft for Witches, Wiccans, and Pagans
Harvest of Gratitude: A Complete Thanksgiving Guide
Yuletide Essentials: A Complete Guide to an Authentic and Magical Christmas
Celestial Smokes: A Cosmic Guide to Cigars and Astrology
Living in Balance: A Comprehensive Survival Guide to Thriving with Diabetes Insipidus
Cosmic Symbiosis: The Venom Zodiac Chronicles
The Cursed Paw of Ambition
Cosmic Symbiosis: The Astrological Venom Journal
Celestial Wonders Unfold: A Stargazer's Guide to the Cosmos (2024-2029)
The Ultimate Black Friday Prepper's Guide: Mastering Shopping Strategies and Savings
Cosmic Sales: The Astrological Guide to Black Friday Shopping
Legends of the Corn Mother and Other Harvest Myths
Whispers of the Harvest: The Corn Mother's Journal
The Evergreen Spellbook
The Doctor Meets the Boogeyman
The White Witch of Rose Hall's SpellBook
The Gingerbread Golem's Shadow: A Study in Sweet Darkness
The Gingerbread Golem Codex: An Academic Exploration of Sweet Myths
The Gingerbread Golem Grimoire: Sweet Magicks and Spells for the Festive Witch
The Curse of the Gingerbread Golem
10-minute Christmas Crafts for kids
Christmas Crisis Solutions: The Ultimate Last-Minute Survival Guide
Gingerbread Golem Recipes: Holiday Treats with a Magical Twist
The Infinite Key: Unlocking Mystical Secrets of the Ages
Enchanted Yule: A Wiccan and Pagan Guide to a Magical and Memorable Season
Dinosaurs of Power: Unlocking Ancient Magick
Astro-Dinos: The Cosmic Guide to Prehistoric Wisdom
Gallifrey's Yule Logs: A Festive Doctor Who Cookbook
The Dino Grimoire: Secrets of Prehistoric Magick
The Gift They Never Knew They Needed
The Gingerbread Golem's Culinary Alchemy: Enchanting Recipes for a Sweetly Dark Feast
A Time Lord Christmas: Holiday Adventures with the Doctor

If you want solar for your home go here: https://www.harborsolar.live/apophisenterprises/

Get Some Tarot cards: https://www.makeplayingcards.com/sell/apophis-occult-shop

Get some shirts: https://www.bonfire.com/store/apophis-shirt-emporium/

<u>**Instagrams:**</u>
@apophis_enterprises,
@apophisbookemporium,
@apophisscardshop
Twitter: @apophisenterpr1
 Tiktok:@apophisenterprise
Youtube: @sg1fan23477, @FiresideRetreatKingdom
Hive: @sg1fan23477
CheeLee: @SG1fan23477

Podcast: Apophis Chat Zone: https://open.spotify.com/show/5zXbr-CLEV2xzCp8ybrfHsk?si=fb4d4fdbdce44dec

Newsletter: https://apophiss-newsletter-27c897.beehiiv.com/